The Aristocratic Universe of
Karen Blixen
DESTINY AND THE DENIAL OF FATE

At the centre of Karen Blixen's stories is the message about the
unwavering significance of art and love. Art could sustain
concepts and thereby materialisation, and it was
imperative to protect love. Karen Blixen's
simple wisdom is that one must be
perfectly clear what is of personal importance,
and then invest everything in that. It never paid to
let matters take their course and try to get off cheaply.
It would be all right to try out one's abilities in various directions
for a while, but sooner or later one was obliged to assemble
one's life in a unity – and she had no hesitation in
identifying the unifying factor, as here in a
letter to a friend: "You have used
yourself well, and have most of the excellent
ingredients at your disposal. – What brings them together?
– What makes a unity out of all of this? And here I can answer you:
love does."

The Aristocratic Universe of
Karen Blixen

DESTINY AND THE DENIAL OF FATE

Frantz Leander Hansen

Translated by Gaye Kynoch

sussex
A C A D E M I C
P R E S S

BRIGHTON • PORTLAND

© Frantz Leander Hansen 2003

The right of Frantz Leander Hansen to be identified as author of this work has been asserted in accordance with the Copyright, Designs and Patents Act 1988.

2 4 6 8 10 9 7 5 3 1

First published in Danish
as *Babette og det aristokratiske univers* [Babette and the Aristocratic Universe],
by C. A. Reitzels Forlag, Copenhagen 1998

First published in English 2003 in Great Britain by
SUSSEX ACADEMIC PRESS
PO Box 2950
Brighton BN2 5SP

and in the United States of America by
SUSSEX ACADEMIC PRESS
920 NE 58th Ave   Suite 300
Portland, Oregon 97213-3786

British Library Cataloguing in Publication Data
A CIP catalogue record for this book is available from the British Library.

Library of Congress Cataloging-in-Publication Data
Hansen, Frantz Leander, 1956–
[Babette og det aristokratiske univers. English]
The aristocratic universe of Karen Blixen : destiny and the denial of
fate / Frantz Leander Hansen.
p. cm.
ISBN (hardcover) 1 903900 32 8 (alk. paper) — ISBN (paperback) 1 903900 33 6
Originally published: Copenhagen : C. A. Reitzel, 1998.
1. Dinesen, Isak, 1885–1962—Criticism and interpretation.
2. Aristocracy (Social class) in literature. I. Title.
PT875.B545 Z695413   2003
839.8'1372—dc21

2002014706

Jacket illustration: Karen Blixen, *c.*1903. Photograph: Carl Sonne.

Typeset and designed by G&G Editorial, Brighton
Printed Bookcraft, Midsomer Norton, Bath
This book is printed on acid-free paper.

Contents

Illustrations

All the photographs of Karen Blixen are in The Department of Maps, Prints and Photographs, The Royal Library, Copenhagen.

COLOUR PLATES: AFTER PAGES 54 AND 86

Karen Blixen: *Still life with bouquet of roses and a book*
Oil on canvas, 40.5 x 35.5 cm, *c.*1916, private collection
Photograph: Ole Woldbye

Karen Blixen: *Sketch of a backyard in Copenhagen*
Pencil and watercolour on paper, 48 x 29 cm, *c.*1903,
The Karen Blixen Museum
Photograph: Bruun Rasmussen Auctioneers of Fine Arts

Karen Blixen: *Young woman with high-necked blouse*
Pencil and charcoal on paper, 41 x 36 cm, 1904–6,
The Karen Blixen Museum
Photograph: Jacob Skov-Hansen

Karen Blixen: *Young girl, profile*
Pencil and charcoal on yellow paper, 61 x 47.5 cm, pre-1914,
The Royal Library, Copenhagen
Photograph: Ole Woldbye

MONOTONE PLATES

Karen Blixen at her desk in Rungstedlund, 1934
PAGE 16

Acknowledgements

Queen Margrethe and Prince Henrik's Foundation, The Danish Literature Centre, Danske Bank's Foundation, G. E. C. Gad's Foundation, The Lademann Foundation and The Raben-Levetzau Foundation have made the translation of this book possible – sincerest thanks for their generous support and interest shown in the project.

I would like to thank my translator, Gaye Kynoch, for proficiency and meticulousness, and for an absorbing collaborative process. Also grateful thanks to Ole Thestrup Pedersen for expert proofreading.

My heartfelt gratitude goes to Anette Halaburt, Else-Marie Leander Hansen, Kim Leander Hansen, Else Hansen, Knud Hansen, Jenny Friberg, Heike Friis, Clara Selborn, Per O. Wegner and Bjarke Kristensen for help and encouragement. I am greatly indebted to Marianne W. Asmussen, Director of The Karen Blixen Museum, Denmark, and to Svend Olufsen, Director of C. A. Reitzel publishers in Copenhagen. My warmest thanks also to Anthony Grahame, Editorial Director, Sussex Academic Press.

To Anette Halaburt

Introduction

Karen Blixen's literary works demonstrate a fascinating interaction between absolute explanation and no meaning. Exploring this fundamental driving force opens the door to Karen Blixen's universe, and reveals that the two currents – the drive for clarity and the pursuit of the dark and secretive – are both in fierce conflict and in total harmony with one another.

Destiny and the denial of fate is an underlying theme in Karen Blixen's entire oeuvre, and follows the absolute meaning/no meaning dichotomy. In Karen Blixen's stories destiny is linked to action, and the notion of destiny applies both to individuals and entire cultures. Conflicts are essentially the outcome of passivity, whereas harmony is achieved through action. In one of her public speeches, Karen Blixen weighed up various approaches to destiny. On the one hand, she maintained that it "will always be the people who, when destiny knocks on the door, immediately open the door, who are loved".[1] On the other hand, Karen Blixen talked about the "destiny-less, destiny-shunning . . . who keep the door closed or open it just a little to usher the guest out", they "perhaps feel easier and are more secure 'out of harm's way', indoors", where, however, "it is not possible to be both truly out of harm's way and to be truly loved".[2] Karen Blixen here touches on a subject that is a principal concern in her stories: the option between being open to or shielded from destiny, both having consequences whichever choice is made. At the same time, there is a hovering image of destiny almost as an actual being, asserting itself with a munificence which is not, however, of a comfortable nature.

Even a single character in one of Karen Blixen's tales can manifest an entire nation. For example, Mr. Clay in "The Immortal Story" (*Anecdotes of Destiny*) can be said to be a personification of England. Or a community, such as the little Norwegian village in "Babette's Feast" (*Anecdotes of Destiny*), can represent the whole of Europe. Throughout her works she poses a critique of civilisation, the extent of which will be quantified in the chapters that follow. It remains to be seen how extensive an openness to destiny she finds in different societies, cultures and religions.

The fundamental currents of absolute explanation and no meaning – which assert a simultaneous divine and demonic character – are invested with flesh and blood in the analysis of the destiny theme, at both the individual and collective level. This will of course involve consideration of the attitudes to historical development to be found in Karen Blixen's works.

An additional and important focal point for the expression of conflict or harmony is the disparity between the *bourgeois* and the *aristocratic*. Here there is not only a potential for illumination, but the discordance provides a means by which to specify and *identify* the various approaches to destiny. Thus in Karen Blixen's works the bourgeois and the aristocratic are fundamentally manifestations of *approaches to life* which are to be found irrespective of time, place – and social class.

The Aristocratic Universe of Karen Blixen demonstrates that the aristocratic philosophy of life is fundamental to all of Karen Blixen's writings. Her views on art are also defined as aristocratic. Understanding the connection between her philosophy of life and her views on art is an essential prerequisite for understanding the structure and purpose of the tales. For example, a description of an aristocratic existence in 'harmony with life's currents' might be painted as being both "infinite and secluded, playful and very grave, safe and dangerous".[3] Such descriptions provide an insight into the cornerstones upon which she builds her stories. And in the stories we will meet the artists she puts to work with these primary colours on their palette.

Karen Blixen deals not only with the grand eternal themes, she is also very concerned with concrete accounts of specific dilemmas. The close correlation between these two planes in her works reveals a scale by which specific dilemmas can be measured. One such measure is: the greater the dissociation from the eternal core, the greater the conflict in a specific historical period.

The aristocratic appears as an approach to life in harmony with the immortal. We can get a feeling of this from the following poetic experience of an aristocratic 'ideal state': "just as dream and reality seemed . . . to have become one, so did the distinction between life and death seem to have been done away with. Dimly he reflected that this state of things would be what was meant by the word immortality. So he looked no more ahead or behind, the hour held him".[4]

This extract, from "Peter and Rosa" (*Winter's Tales*), throws up the question of the role played in Karen Blixen's works by the perception of primordial forces. In other words: what significance is assigned to *wild-*

ness? In this respect Africa finds its inherent status. Discussion extends to the relationship between wildness and cultural evolution – not only in Africa, but also in Europe. Karen Blixen presents radically different pictures of the two continents' administration of wildness and culture – and this leads to an uncompromising critique of outsiders' endeavours to 'civilise' Africa. At the same time, the 'African' element to the oeuvre must be ascribed a broader significance in which European conduct in Africa is a picture of the administration of aristocratic roots *in* Europe.

If the idea of immortality is essential to the interpretation of life presented by Karen Blixen then it must also be central to her approach to art. The implication is a portrait of an author who makes great demands of literature: it must fulfil an eternal need and be made of immortal substance. When hefty demands are made, much must be left behind. Thus one task in the pages that follow will be to investigate the forms of expression Karen Blixen wished to do away with via her immortal art.

II

"Babette's Feast" is a playful and very grave tale, as lucid and ambiguous as Hemingway. It is often claimed that "Babette's Feast" belongs to the lighter, even 'popular' branch of Karen Blixen's work. Its prime quality is that the tale both can belong here – and is also so much more. The story is something of a Trojan horse, concealing an unexpected artillery. From an aristocratic point of view, "Babette's Feast" can be placed at the heart of the oeuvre, as a focus for the threads to be unravelled in all her literary work. The tale actually *is* 'the hub of events', in that it is here that the old and the new worlds collide decisively; and it is here that, in historical perspective, the hour of destiny has come for the aristocratic outlook. "Babette's Feast" will be discussed in relation to the entire oeuvre, taking into consideration specific circumstances in Karen Blixen's life.

In Karen Blixen's case, biographical details – her background and daily life – contain relevant circumstances necessary for a full under-standing of her preoccupations in her writing. The tales can in no way be reduced to autobiography, but biographical elements add profoundly to an understanding of them. Further, and most importantly, Karen Blixen would not have drawn on her personal experience had she not seen universal elements therein.

Part I – Karen Blixen's Works – presents Karen Blixen's oeuvre, which also serves as preparation for the in-depth analyses to follow. Representative stories from each collection are selected for comment, in order to give an overall picture of the themes found in the works, which comprise short stories, a novel, a play, a literary memoir (*Out of Africa*), poetry and essays. Karen Blixen was also a painter and a frequent visitor to art galleries; an appraisal will therefore be made of how her attitude to painting influenced her writing.

Part II – When Destiny Comes Calling – includes "Babette's Feast" as part of *Anecdotes of Destiny*; other stories in this collection also shed light on the destiny theme. A comparative study of "The Ring" and "Babette's Feast" demonstrates that the tales represent two different approaches to destiny, which are dominant in the entire collection of her works.

Part III – Life and Tale – presents biographical elements and an exposition of Karen Blixen's world of ideas as expressed in letters and other records. Her letters are referred to throughout in order to shed light on her life and work. The most recently published collection of Karen Blixen's letters, *Karen Blixen in Denmark: Letters, 1931–62*, provides a new understanding of the author and her writing. The collection was published in 1996, but has yet to be translated in published form to English; however, central aspects of these new letters are discussed in the chapters that follow, and the major insights of the letters are supported here by English translations.

III

Karen Blixen wrote most of her stories in both English and Danish. She did not translate them, but retold them in the other language. Her usual method was to write the tales in English first and thereafter retell them in Danish. The outcome is a fascinating bilingualism in which, on a number of occasions, she has added to the Danish version. If Karen Blixen had a new idea during the Danish retelling, she happily incorporated it as a natural variant of the story. In *The Aristocratic Universe of Karen Blixen*, quotations from additions to the Danish versions have been translated into English. The selection of such quotations has been based on the significance of the passages for the interpretation of the texts. But, hopefully, English-language readers will also be introduced to new aspects of Karen Blixen's works.

PART I

Karen Blixen's Works

Truth and Creation

Early writing and painting

Karen Christentze Dinesen was born to Ingeborg and Wilhelm Dinesen in 1885 at the family home of Rungstedlund, a spacious house on the coast road north of Copenhagen. She took the name Blixen on her marriage in 1914 to Baron Bror von Blixen-Finecke. Her father had been an officer in the Danish army, later enlisting in the French army, but in 1879 he acquired the large estate of which Rungstedlund was a part. Besides being a landowner, Wilhelm Dinesen was active in politics and had written a number of books, including *Paris under Communen* (*Paris During the Commune*, 1872), *Jagtbreve* (*Letters from the Hunt*, 1889) and *Nye jagtbreve* (*New Letters from the Hunt*, 1892). Wilhelm Dinesen wrote under the pseudonym Boganis (meaning 'little hazelnut'), a name he had been given by the native Indians amongst whom he lived in North America from 1872 to 1874. Karen Blixen's father came from the country estate of Katholm near Grenå in Jutland, and her mother, née Westenholz, came from another country estate, Mattrup near Horsens, also in Jutland.

Long before the Dinesen family took over Rungstedlund it had been an inn, and the great lyric poet Johannes Ewald had lived there from 1773 to 1775. Unusually for the times, Ewald had attempted to live solely from the proceeds of his writing. His financial and social circumstances were therefore poor, added to which he suffered from a rheumatic complaint and a great fondness for drinking. His mother consequently took control of his affairs, one of her measures being to place him in exile at Rungsted Inn. He wrote the beautiful poem "Rungsteds Lyksaligheder" (The Joys of Rungsted, 1775) whilst living there – about a poet's liberation in his encounter with nature, also representative of the 'female'. One of Ewald's most original tales, "Mester Synaals Fortelling" (Master Tailor Synaal's Tale, 1780), is ahead of its time in its dreamlike quality and by having the tale itself as the theme. He also wrote plays, and in *Adam og Ewa* (*Adam and Eve*, 1769) God and Satan are seen working *together* to drive Adam and Eve out of Paradise. Karen Blixen not only found inspiration in the myth of Ewald, which lived on at Rungstedlund, but also in his writings, which she valued highly.

There was an artistic heritage to uphold at Rungstedlund, and four of Ingeborg and Wilhelm Dinesen's five children displayed an all-round talent for the arts. As a child Karen Blixen started to draw, paint and write. She drew landscapes, figures from fairy tales and illustrations for her own and other writers' stories; she drew and painted portraits and flower pieces, and later on, when living in Africa, she concentrated primarily on portraits of the indigenous people. Some of the drawings she did when young are signed Peter Lawless!* She received formal training by attending Charlotte Sode and Julie Meldahl's drawing school in Copenhagen from 1902 to 1903, a prerequisite for attending the Royal Academy of Fine Arts, where she studied from 1903 to 1906. In 1910 she attended Simon and Ménard's art school in Paris, and in 1925 she took lessons with the painter Bertha Dorph. Karen Blixen hoped for an independent career as a painter – an ambition she held right up until her last years in Africa. However, despite undoubted talent, on her return to Denmark in 1931 she put painting in oils aside, and from that time on she only made the occasional drawing. She acknowledged her limitations as a painter and instead concentrated on developing fully as a writer. Perhaps she could have pursued her desire to develop her talent as a painter if circumstances had been more favourable; as a woman she received no encouragement from family or society to follow an independent career, and in *Karen Blixen's Drawings* (*Karen Blixens Tegninger*, 1969) she says that Bertha Dorph was the only teacher who had tried to encourage her progress.[1] The rest of the teaching she received had been extremely traditional, with no reference to new trends of the time.

In Africa, Karen Blixen saw an originality that she regretted not being able to turn to account as a painter, as she tells us indirectly: "A great artist who had come to East Africa at the time when I came there myself, would have been able to astonish the world, as Gauguin did from Tahiti and Dominica, with unknown colours and lines in the human body."[2] She had a comprehensive knowledge of the art of painting, and it was an art form that had great significance for her perception of the world and thus for her depiction of it: "I owe painting even far more. For me it has constantly revealed the true nature of the real world. I have always had difficulty in finding my way into a landscape unless a great artist has given me the key."[3] Painting was the discipline that inspired her most, and could even be directly motivating: "I could name quite specific paintings which for me have been converted into quite specific

---

*A name possibly inspired by Will Lawless, a character in Robert Louis Stevenson's novel *The Black Arrow* (1884).

stories."[4] Karen Blixen goes a step further in defining the influence of painting – by placing it alongside music she simply cancels the boundaries between the art forms: "For me there is no actual difference between them: writing is also pictures and tones."[5] This is a precise characterisation of her own writing. Karen Blixen's endeavours as a painter and her study of works by other artists left a very vivid impression – the painter's fine sense for colour and line attained its full scope in her writing. She wrote pictorially, in the best sense of the word, as can be seen from the abundant and wonderful descriptions of nature in her works.

During her childhood and adolescence Karen Blixen wrote poems, plays and stories. A poem written when she was possibly only 15 sets out a theme that was to remain central throughout her career: the fertile interplay between the divine and the demonic: "As lovely flowers root in stone and marsh / so perfection grows from torment and tribulation / Repose and light will blossom like roses / from storm and disquiet, darkness, struggle and longing . . . What does darkness say and what does light teach? / Listen, for sorrow and joy have the same voice."[6]

At Rungstedlund, with her siblings and friends, Karen Blixen presented several plays that she had written herself. In *The Life and Destiny of Isak Dinesen*, for example, there is a photograph of the performers in the play *Pride Goes Before a Fall* (*Hovmod staar for Fald*), which she wrote as an 11-year-old.[7] Unfortunately the script has been lost. In 1904 she wrote the marionette play *The Revenge of Truth* (*Sandhedens Hævn*), which she reworked several times and eventually published in 1926, at which point she made persistent efforts to get it produced. In a letter from Africa she gives detailed instructions as to the set, costumes and music. As a help to visualising the characters, she refers to paintings in which they could have featured![8] However, no production materialised at this time, so Karen Blixen gave it a role in her story "The Roads Around Pisa" from *Seven Gothic Tales* (1934). The play was later produced professionally, including productions at the Royal Danish Theatre, on Danish television and as an opera.

The Revenge of Truth is very untraditional. Karen Blixen was fully aware of this, describing it as "theatre multiplied, or a caricature of theatre"[9] and as being "not subject to the usual rules".[10] In the play every naturalistic illusion about watching a slice of reality is undermined, as the performers make it perfectly clear that we are dealing with fiction. In a totally modern fashion, they discuss their own roles and the drama in which they are playing a part. The extremely self-referential quality of the play establishes the theme that is a mainstay in many of Karen Blixen's stories – the nature of the arts themselves. The self-referential aspect is summed up when one of the performers says he will be writing a review of *The Revenge of Truth* the next day; this also has the effect of making the play seem new at every performance. The relationship between art and experience is discussed, and the focus on roles and masks also raises the issue of identity and the roles we all play in our lives. Now and then the performers turn contemptuously on the audience – the 'audience' also representing mere spectators to life. The 'dramatist' himself is claimed to have a role in the play, during the course of which he declares himself satisfied with everything apart from his own character, which he cannot resolve; he abandons the attempt as "the terrible fate of the artist is that I can't do that".[11] The writer as a person must be kept out of it, otherwise the plot will be undermined. The witch, Amiane, acts as soothsayer, and at the outset she puts on record that in a marionette play the essential thing is to "keep the author's idea clear. Aye, drive it to its utmost consequence . . . this is the real happiness."[12] Her comment is directed at the performers, but as she states that everyone is acting a part in a marionette play, it is also directed at the audience: one has to be aware of all elements of 'creation' and take full advantage of its potential. If one does not do this, one is living a lie, and the 'author's idea' is the truth that wreaks revenge on those who refuse to recognise it. Amiane – the witch – weaves a spell by means of which she exposes these lies and brings the truth to light. The play unmasks those who renounce life, but according to Amiane even these people long for the witchcraft that will enable them to live a true – and that means complete – life, in which all their potential will be fulfilled. Karen Blixen's conception of truth is very concrete, as is also evident in a letter from Africa:

> *"The longer I live, I think that what matters most to me is truth; I do not think that anyone can be happy except in conditions that, consciously or instinctively, they have chosen as the expression of their true nature, and many of the difficulties of one's youth are the result of one's having chosen or had ambition about things that one admires theoretically, and that 'must be' right for one too, but that in reality one does not love or belong among. Most people probably have quite a lot to overcome or resign themselves to in order truly to recognize, and acknowledge, their own true nature."[13]*

Karen Blixen mostly set her stories in the 18th or 19th centuries, but *The Revenge of Truth* is one of the few works to take place in the 20th century. The turn of the century and the transition to the modern era are emphasised at several points in the story, and it is pointed out that modernity offends against 'creation' and consequently makes it difficult for people to find the truth: "Oh no, the times, even the century itself, must change before it is worth living."[14]

Juvenilia, in the form of stories and poems, are collected in *Osceola* (1962), and two early stories appear in *Carnival – Entertainments and Posthumous Tales.*[15] In her youth, Karen Blixen wrote under the pseudonym Osceola – the name of the chief of a North American Indian tribe – a man her father had admired and named his dog after.

Karen Blixen published her first work in 1907, the tale "The Hermits", in which we meet the young newly-weds Lucie and Eugène Vandamm, who in 1779 go to stay on a deserted island in order to give Eugène peace and quiet to write a book. While Eugène isolates himself in his study, Lucie's own isolation on the island intensifies as she is left to her dreamworld and the forces of nature. We see the unhappy consequences of the 'male' and the 'female' being isolated from one another. Eugène only employs "his external being",[16] he is a rational man who only respects dry facts. As the book he is writing is based on this one-sidedness, it is doomed from the outset. Lucie is facing the same destiny in that she sinks into a pure dreamworld where time and consciousness are suspended, finally to 'drown' in the boundless ocean.

At the same time "The Hermits" depicts the fundamental conditions for existence described through the natural elements, which starkly confront the inhabitants of a deserted island far removed from civilisation. For Karen Blixen, nature is not just wonderful descriptions of scenery, but also that which is given from nature's hand – the inevitable. In "The Hermits" it is the earth that is changed by human hand, whilst the heavens and the sea are the unalterable conditions providing the setting for human endeavour. The heavens *and* the sea are the creation within which the human can flourish:

> "*The earth is the human element between the elements, the air is the divine, the sea is Satan. The earth is inconstant . . . the heavens and the sea are constant . . . In its eternal, high clarity the air is the symbol of all explained, pure, blessed, in its eternal restlessness the sea is the symbol and expression of the excluded, the craving, demonic, forever unsettled . . . In the world in which we move, the sky, earth and sea are brothers, indivisible, one and yet three, blended in an eternal and divine harmony.*"[17]

In Karen Blixen's writings things always go badly for the person who excludes the divine or the demonic aspect of existence where these forces are reflected in the individual in the form of the masculine and feminine. "The Hermits" demonstrates that there are early stories which bear comparison with the later and more famous works.

Another early tale, "The de Cats Family" (1909), is a bitter and amusing satire on the bourgeois philosophy that puts up barriers and shuts doors. Many of Karen Blixen's tales maintain that respectable bourgeois families *must* have black sheep in whom all misery has been concentrated, and "The de Cats Family" is a whole tale on this theme. The 'bourgeois' is here characterised through the airing of vice, thus also creating a contrast to virtue, which thereby stands out even more clearly. The point is also a simple one: the bourgeoisie's existence depends on the impression of being better than others.

Encounter with the Primary

Accounts of Africa

Her arrival in Africa in 1914 at the age of 28 fulfilled Karen Blixen's long-held wish to liberate herself from her childhood home. *Letters from Africa, 1914–1931* is a fascinating correspondence covering the seventeen years in Kenya during which Karen Blixen ran a coffee farm – at first with her husband, but following the breakdown of their marriage in the early 1920s she managed the farm alone. The letters bear witness to her marital problems and difficulties in running the farm, but her personal searching develops – especially when problems on the farm pile up – into a revolt against her childhood and adolescence at Rungstedlund. Her experience of Africa's nature and culture dominates the letters, which show a passionate interest in everything to do with the indigenous people, from their rich imagination to details of their everyday routines. At the time it was very unusual for a white woman to show any interest in the 'natives' beyond their capacity for work. Life on the farm was outgoing and very busy, but in her letters Karen Blixen was able to concentrate her thoughts, also about literature and painting, and now and then there are whole 'essays' about problems of existence in general.

Returning to Denmark in 1931, Karen Blixen used her experiences in Kenya to write *Out of Africa* (1937), which can best be described as a literary memoir as she also applies the expression and freedoms of fiction. In an aristocratic way, Karen Blixen keeps herself in the background in order to paint an expansive portrait of Africa and the people she met there, which had indeed been her clear intention: "I do not want to be in any way the heroine of the book, it should be a book of Africa."[18] *Out of Africa* contains magnificent descriptions of landscape and animal life, but its main purpose was to provide a picture of African culture before it was too late. The fateful impact of the encounter with European culture plays its unavoidable role in the book, and there were no illusions about her grounds for writing it: "I will sing the native world's swan song."[19]

Whereas the letters are the direct and contemporary account of Karen Blixen's life in Kenya and *Out of Africa* is a literary reworking of material that was still very much alive to her, *Shadows on the Grass* (1960) is a cooler reflection on Africa, written in essay form after an interval of thirty years. The book comprises four essays in which Karen Blixen reiterates the themes from her earlier accounts, but adds experiences from the intervening period and relates what had since happened to the people she left behind in Africa.

Fantastical Transformation

Seven Gothic Tales

As a buffer against the intense problems she faced at the end of her stay in Africa, Karen Blixen wrote two stories, "The Roads Around Pisa" and "The Old Chevalier", and she started a third, "The Monkey", before returning home to Denmark.[20] Thus she was well on the way to assembling *Seven Gothic Tales*, which was published in 1934 under the pseudonym Isak Dinesen, a name she used frequently from then on. With 'Dinesen', Karen Blixen denotes her roots in her father's aristocratic universe; 'Isak' comes from the biblical story about Sarah, who learns as a very old woman that she is to have a child, which makes her laugh out loud, and she names her son Isak (Isaac in English), meaning 'laughter' or ''the one who laughs'. In choosing this particular name, Karen Blixen indicates the origins of her tales in myth, and she stresses the significance of 'laughter', which in the tales is indicative of liberating recognition. Her friend Gustav Mohr asks in a letter: "Why Isak? Is it Kasi backwards?"[21] We have no reply from Karen Blixen, but it is likely that she had also thought about 'kasi', which means 'energy' in Swahili.

Whilst working on *Seven Gothic Tales*, Karen Blixen remarked that they are "in the manner of the 'Short Stories' of the beginning of the last century", but that they also strike "a kind of new note in short stories".[22] The remark is interesting because it shows a conscious endeavour to write in the classic and modern styles at one and the same time – a significant motivation being Karen Blixen's conviction that it was necessary to make it modern to add the classical element to the contemporary.

Seven Gothic Tales was first published in English and subsequently in Danish. By writing in English, Karen Blixen sought a wider audience than just Danish readers, but it was also because of her belief that *Seven Gothic Tales* would not evoke a response in the Danish mentality: "I still believe that the Danish readership, which has not the slightest tradition for this kind of fantastical, – or <u>nonsense</u>, – type of literature, will ask, with some indignation: what is this all about?"[23] Yet Karen Blixen *wanted* to be read in Denmark and have a place in Danish literature, but for this to happen she believed that a change in mentality was necessary – to which she contributed with her attempt to give Danish literature a new lease of life. The choice of the fantastic as expressive form was also motivated by her view that it was badly needed, not just in the Danish but also in the greater part of European culture. In a letter from Africa, when she had started work on *Seven Gothic Tales*, she writes: "I think that this whole age has a longing for fantasy and the marvelous in art . . . "[24] The tales had their springboard in Africa in more than one respect, as there is no doubt that she was inspired by her experience of the fantasy and superstition which were a natural element of everyday African life.

At the beginning of the first tale, "The Roads Around Pisa", Count von Schimmelmann recalls his childhood visit to the mirror-room of the Panoptikon in Copenhagen: "where you see yourself reflected, to the right and the left, in the ceiling and even on the floor, in a hundred glasses each of which distorts and perverts your face and figure in a different way – shortening, lengthening, broadening, compressing their shape, and still keeping some sort of likeness – and thought how much this was like real life."[25] Herein is also an invitation to the reader to step into the tales as if into a mirror-room and thereby see oneself from new and surprising angles. At the same time the reader is given a characterisation of the tales to come: like a mirror-room they turn reality upside down, distort and contort, but with the purpose of looking deeper into that reality, so that reality will indeed be seen as fantastic. Karen Blixen would undoubtedly have been happy to endorse the definition of reality proposed by Dostoevsky : "What most people regard as fantastic and lacking in universality, *I* hold to be the inmost essence of truth. Arid observation of everyday trivialities I have long ceased to regard as realism – it is quite the reverse."[26]

By employing the fantastic element, Karen Blixen's intention was to provide a more comprehensive representation of reality, and she considered an open and free imagination to be an important agent for this purpose. As the Cardinal says in "The Deluge at Norderney", every individual at times considers "the idea of creating a world himself."[27] When one comes to grips with this, the project will only succeed if there is no calling to account and stopping half-way – as the Cardinal's advice to the artist continues: "Be not afraid of absurdity; do not shrink from the fantastic. Within a dilemma, choose the most unheard-of, the most dangerous, solution."[28] This is not just a piece of advice for artists, but also for connoisseurs of the art of living.

In *Seven Gothic Tales* Karen Blixen makes extensive use of a favourite narrative technique: to let the participant characters tell each other stories, by means of which the tale becomes a complexity of stories slotting into one another like a Russian doll. The individual story is augmented by the others, as the stories lend one another significance and the multiple stories form one expansive tale. From the multiplicity emerges unity, but at the same time the multiplicity is accentuated by the underlying point of view that no story is complete – a story cannot tell the reader everything about a character, because the picture of that character changes as soon as he or she appears in a new story.

This approach – a multiplicity of stories in a single tale – applies to Karen Blixen's entire body of work, in which the multiplicity of tales relate to one another to an extent that now and then they seem like segments in a cyclical novel. Added to this, Karen Blixen, like a painter, continually refines certain motifs, and a minor theme in one tale becomes the principal theme in the next or vice versa. In large measure, we are therefore presented with the eternal reappearance of the same themes. We can go a step further: Karen Blixen's characteristic incorporation of myth and other literature into her tales is also an expression of the 'stories within stories' forming one expansive tale. World literature is a unity of limitless stories, which are also a repetition of the immortal stories that are forever relevant.

In the choice of the situations in which Karen Blixen lets her characters tell each other stories, the 'fantastic' atmosphere is already established. There are the characters in "The Dreamers" who tell their

Karen Blixen at her desk in Rungstedlund, 1934

stories at night and at sea under full sail. Normality and logic are suspended, night is the time for dreams, and the sea is also the territory of
the subconscious and irrational. There are the characters in "The Deluge
at Norderney" who tell their stories whilst confined to a hayloft, their
lives in grave danger from the water rising all around them. This is also
an example of how Karen Blixen places her characters in 'extreme circumstances', where they pass judgment upon themselves and can speak
their minds bluntly. A common feature of Karen Blixen's tales is the Day
of Judgment taking place in miniature: it is not a case of witnessing isolated segments of life, but of taking stock of *whole* destinies.

The extreme circumstances force the central question of identity to
its limit: who am I? The tales give the clear answer that there is no fixed
identity, which the characters always acknowledge with relief, as they
have felt imprisoned in the artificial notion of the immovable 'I'.
Freedom is found in the multi-personality, and here we have the theme
of changing masks. Unity in the individual comes from the ability to play
the multiple roles that collectively make up one's *substance*. For Karen
Blixen absence of one fixed identity does not preclude substance and
personality, as this is attained by living out every facet of one's nature.
This renders one capable of forming a notion of 'self', and one can
thereby *create* one's 'self'. Lack of character is, on the contrary, found in
people who attempt to construct a single, specific 'face', or who only
imitate others. There is a parody of this in "The Deluge at Norderney",
with an inset tale in which everyone follows the example of a certain
'man of fashion', resulting in the annihilation of their individual
substance, a circumstance that could have come straight out of Johannes
Ewald's "Master Tailor Synaal's Tale".

Calypso in "The Deluge at Norderney" is the keenly-drawn emblem
of that category of women in Karen Blixen's works who have an extreme
problem with the issue of identity because they are kept in total ignorance of their femininity. This ignorance is presented with crystal-clear
symbolism in Calypso's upbringing in an out-and-out male world: living
with an uncle who only surrounds himself with young boys and who
brings Calypso up like a boy. When her female form begins to develop,
he brutally rejects her, thereby revealing her "non-existence".[29] In order
to conform to her surroundings, she decides to cut off her hair and
breasts! But she is saved by Greek mythology when she comes across an
intensely sensual painting, which has Dionysian adoration of naked
nymphs as its central motif. The nymph in Calypso steps forward – in
one fell swoop she becomes aware of her desirable femininity, and she

escapes to freedom. Her ignorance is emphasised by her belief that the figures in the painting are real beings, but this has another significance about which she is right: the mythological picture is also a concentrated *true* manifestation of her femininity. Calypso's ignorance is not merely dangerous unenlightenment, but also the pure mind to which the notion of indecency does not occur. She looks at the picture without a shred of moral condemnation.

Athena in "The Monkey" is cast from the same mould as Calypso. She is inordinately mannish, this being again a clear indication of the absence of love and femininity. Her "maiden grave"[30] would have remained sealed had not the only way out of a hopeless situation for Boris, a lieutenant in the Royal Guards, been marriage to Athena. The matchmaker is Boris's aunt, a prioress who, with her ability to transform herself into a monkey, has the necessary means: as a monkey she is able to bring out the animal in Boris, enabling him to penetrate Athena's armour and evoke the animal in her as well. The force of nature liberates. By surrendering to his nature "as a coast sinks around a ship which takes the open sea, so did all the worries of his life sink around this release of all his being".[31] His brain is disengaged, and although he had not previously had much experience of fury, he now "gave his heart up to the rapture of it. His soul laughed . . . "[32] Boris is not alone − Athena is also in one of the "situations in life, when reliance on rationality and good common sense no longer applies",[33] as Karen Blixen says in a letter about the necessity of exploring every possible avenue when confronted with extreme circumstances. The destruction of the mannishness in which Athena is armoured is total, as she is transformed into a skeleton and thus into her *fundamental* being; as a skeleton with distinct monkey features to her death's-head, the animal in her comes to the forefront.

The tale presents Athena with an image of the Wendish goddess of love, Faru, who appears in pictures with a beautiful woman's face on the front and with a grinning monkey on the reverse. Athena shows an intuitive understanding by asking how one can know which is the front and which the back! Athena herself ends with the possibility of having the same doubleness as Faru: to be a beautiful woman *because* she is simultaneously a monkey.

In Karen Blixen's writings there is a clear message about the freedom to be achieved when the animal aspect of a person comes into its own. As will be seen, the animal also contributes to liberate Lise in "The Ring". Similarly, the positive aspect of wildness is often emphasised in the letters, mainly in general terms, but in the following passage Karen Blixen discusses it with specific reference to "The Monkey":

> *"Should one look for a deeper meaning in the story, it would probably be this: when human affairs become particularly complicated or in complete disarray, then let the monkey step in. In the Closter Boris receives monkey-counsel and monkey-support; when, through this, at least a way out and a light in the darkness is perceived, the Prioress comes back and resumes her place. The monkey has obviously been following a path of crime, which the Prioress does not want stepped on, but in its resolution there is salvation for Boris and, it should be read, also the promise of a more human happiness for Athena."* [54]

The same advice about monkey-support, incidentally, is given in Peter Høeg's *The Woman and the Ape* (*Kvinden og aben*, 1996).

There is great understanding, even sympathy, for offenders – lawbreakers – in Karen Blixen's works. The monkey actually urges Boris to ravish Athena. In the powerful tale "The Wine of the Tetrarch", which is an inset in "The Deluge at Norderney", the great sinner Barrabas meets the Apostle Peter. Barrabas is strong and proud – *he* does not need help to carry a cross. He has intrepidly risked his life to save a friend, whereas Peter three times denies knowing Jesus. Peter is portrayed with profound irony; he is egoistically preoccupied with his own salvation, and his salvation of others is called the duty to be a fisher of men. Unlike Barrabas, Peter is frightened and lacks potency. The contrast between the divine and the worldly is explicit: whilst Peter is distressed about the crucified Jesus, Barrabas is angry that, in the wake of the Crucifixion, an earthquake has ruined a stolen hogshead of wine he has buried under a cedar on the mountainside! Barrabas is, moreover, very interested in the wine drunk at the Last Supper, but his interest is purely in terms of the quality of taste, demonstrating his own one-sidedness, whereas Peter is only concerned with the sacred aspect of the wine. Karen Blixen has recorded a brilliant retelling of "The Wine of the Tetrarch", [35] and it is the best of her many recordings in this genre, which she valued highly. She did not read aloud from stories she had already written, as she was of the firm opinion that what was written down should be read; the oral telling of a story should be approached freely, not learnt by heart, or you should tell a completely new story.

Aristocratic Conduct of Life and Bourgeois Lifelessness

Winter's Tales

Shortly after finishing *Out of Africa*, Karen Blixen began writing *Winter's Tales*, which was published in 1942. The title is taken from Shakespeare's play *The Winter's Tale* (1611), but undoubtedly also refers to the wintry conditions in Denmark during World War II. Of all Karen Blixen's books, *Winter's Tales* is the one that is most concerned with Danish subjects.

Thus the tale "Sorrow-Acre" is based on an old Danish legend of the same name and takes place on a country estate in Denmark around the year 1780. With his modern, liberal and humane ideas, the young man Adam is faced with his uncle, the lord of the manor, who upholds the old, aristocratic ideals. Adam's defence of the Nordic gods and the old lord's defence of the Greek gods illustrates the contrast between them. Adam asserts that the Nordic gods possessed the *human* virtues; they were righteous, trustworthy and benevolent, whereas the Greek gods were mean, capricious and treacherous. From the old lord's point of view, the Nordic gods were able to behave as they did because it was left to the Jotuns – darker powers – to be treacherous, whereas the Greek gods' power was monistic and therefore more arduous, but superior: they did not merely exercise virtue, but also took responsibility for the dark side of life, which nevertheless made them *all*-powerful, with the whole universe at their disposal. The old lord's point of view, to which he conforms in *his* exercise of power, is in complete accordance with the central concept in Karen Blixen's works: the unity of the divine and the demonic.

Adam uses the negatively-charged word 'capricious', but in a positive assessment of 'Greek' power it would be called 'unpredictable', which in Karen Blixen's concept is another word for the demonic. As part of life pure and simple, the unpredictable element has to be a component of genuine discharge of power; for instance, Karen Blixen says that the 'native' could not respect a ruler who did not have this trait: "Amongst the qualities that he will be looking for in a master . . . or in God, imagination, I believe, comes high up in the list. It may be on the strength of such a taste, that the Caliph Haroun al Raschid maintains, to the hearts of Africa and Arabia, his position as an ideal ruler; with him nobody knew what to expect next, and you did not know where you had him."[36] Haroun al Raschid readily acted incognito, and among the names he used was Albondocani, which Karen Blixen used as the title of a planned novel!

Similarly, Adam's charge of 'meanness' is converted into the Greek gods' management of life's demonically hard, but inevitable, reality. It also seems cruel when the old lord ironically discourses on human right-eousness and benevolence. But, in Karen Blixen's concept of power, the 'inhuman' is to be understood as the general and impersonal, which must be in control; thus power is based on the eternal values. If a ruler allows himself to be moved by righteousness and benevolence, and thereby individual considerations, he is pulled down to the human plane where he does not belong. There are many instances in Karen Blixen's works where it is emphasised that, in order to preserve his overall perspective and his impersonal power, a ruler must *separate* himself from those he rules over. This is summed up in "The Deluge at Norderney": there should be no "moral attitude" in a god or a ruler, on the contrary it is liberating if they do not "give a pin for our commandments".[37] This is a forceful assertion that authority should not restrict, but, without preju-dice, keep the endless opportunities of life open – which will not be the case if one rules from an ethos contrived by people and typical of a specific era.

Matters come to a head between Adam and his uncle when the old lord sets the peasant woman and widow, Anne-Marie, to mow an entire rye-field on her own between sunrise and sunset; by so doing she can save her son, Goske, from being brought before the district judge to face the charge of arson – which would result in the loss of her son. Adam considers his uncle's conduct to be despotic; to the old lord it is a completely natural course of action. Anne-Marie finishes her work the very second before the sun goes down, and as she sinks to her knees, dying from exhaustion, the old lord gives Goske leave to tell his mother that he is free.

This would seem to be a story about brutal, despotic exercise of power, but Adam is only in the right as long as we stay on the surface. In the same way, it is a case of surface interpretation when – as in the tendency represented by the writer Aage Henriksen – the old lord's conduct in relation to Anne-Marie is solely construed as tyrannical "abuse of power".[38] To Karen Blixen, this is of course a matter of historical recording of the aristocracy's struggle to preserve its authority at a time when bourgeois democracy and concepts of the rights of the individual surfaced. But, notwithstanding that in "Sorrow-Acre" a sigh is heaved in the face of a world being taken over by bourgeois attitudes, on a deeper level the tale moves away from the historical interpretation and becomes a depiction of attitudes to life. Criticism of the lord of the manor fades, his seemingly despotic conduct becomes a symbolic representation of an aristocratic attitude to life, shunning time, place – and rank. This picture also admits the bond between the old lord and Anne-Marie, who are indeed only segregated on the surface. The destinies of Anne-Marie and the old lord augment one another, and eventually Adam becomes part of the alliance.

The lord of the manor has married a very young girl who had been intended as the bride for his son, who died before the wedding could take place; the old lord would therefore ensure the continuation of his lineage. The connection between the lord of the manor and Anne-Marie is the simple fact that Goske was the only person the old lord's son ever liked when he was a child. They were playmates, as is also said of Adam and the old lord's son; it is thus probable that this bond also exists between Adam and Goske.

The uncle's marriage seemingly eliminates Adam from inheriting the estate. But various circumstances make it clear to Adam that he nevertheless has a role in the perpetuation of the family line. At the beginning of the tale he delights in his uncle's garden, which "is as fresh as the garden of Eden . . . it looked as if here nothing had changed, but all was what it used to be".[39] The country estate is rooted in eternal values, but there is also cause for the old lord to enjoin Adam to eat freely from the trees in Paradise, by which he holds out the prospect of an Eve. The subsequent description of the young wife makes it clear that the marriage has not borne fruit in the form of the anticipated heir. And having spent some time observing Anne-Marie's struggle in the rye-field to give new life to her son, Adam suddenly understands the connection, abandons his dispute with his uncle and goes to his aunt in the manor house – there to take his uncle's place and put new life into the lineage. Adam's conquest is not an abuse of his aunt and a rebellion against his uncle, as Aage Henriksen suggests;[40] on the contrary, it happens in complete accordance with their wishes.

Adam's father died young, and his uncle took over the father's role, thus enabling Adam to fulfil the 'filial' duty of perpetuating the family line. Furthermore, a gypsy-woman had read his hand and foretold that his son would succeed to the estate. Adam's initial detachment from the lord of the manor's milieu is not only for noble-minded democratic reasons, but more because in England he had "met with greater wealth and magnificence",[41] and a love affair with an English lady of such high rank that she would think his uncle's estate a mere toy-farm makes him look down on his uncle. Adam's conversion therefore also involves his acknowledgement of egoistic motives and the particular distinction of the impersonal aristocratic perspective. But this perspective has always held sway over him: at the very outset he is attracted to the idea of giving up "individual wealth and happiness to serve the greater ideals".[42] Adam's denunciation of his uncle is not least a manifestation of his desire to follow the current of the *times*: bourgeois ideology and therefore also personal advantage. That Adam makes his aunt pregnant, *because* he nevertheless identifies with his uncle's perspective, and not because he is taking revenge on a tyrant by cuckolding him, is made plain by his reflections towards the end of the tale. He has just shown his understanding of Anne-Marie's and therefore his uncle's struggle by breaking "off a few ears of rye"[43] himself, when in his thoughts he sees "the ways of life . . . as a twined and tangled design. . . . Life and death, happiness and woe, the past and the present, were interlaced within the pattern . . . out of the contrasting elements concord arose . . . So might now, to the woman in the rye-field, her ordeal be a triumphant procession . . . the unity of things . . . had been disclosed to him today . . . Anne-Marie and he were both in the hands of destiny . . . ".[44] This is unambiguously 'Greek' and 'aristocratic', sanctioning his uncle's conduct in relation to Anne-Marie.

Events in the rye-field and the manor serve a common purpose: Anne-Marie's and the lord's efforts are united in concern to perpetuate the family line. The old lord has made it possible for Anne-Marie to save Goske, and Anne-Marie's feat secures the lord an heir, as it is her endeavour that motivates Adam. What is said of Anne-Marie – that her son means life itself to her – also applies to the lord of the manor. Whatever the characters in the tale might harbour of personal feelings for one another, or for looking after their own skin, is subordinate to the family lineage, to the overall picture. This is aristocratic conduct, displayed not only by the lord, his wife and, eventually, Adam, but also by Anne-Marie and Goske. Similarly, Goske selflessly hazards his life for one he loves by refusing to inform against a married woman he was with at the time of the arson.

The aristocratic becomes an attitude to life for both high and low.

Anne-Marie's action is aristocratic. She sets aside considerations of her own life in order to give life to her son (the family line), and it is said that she acts without fear and would not stop even if asked to — that would be a violation of her honour. Anne-Marie would react like "the true fighting bull" in "The Deluge at Norderney", who in anger would attack "the master of ceremonies" if "out of compassion" orders should be given to abandon the bullfight. The bull will not be prevented from being "known for many years as that black bull which put up such a fine fight".[45] Like Anne-Marie, it gets its memorial; it is the feat that counts. But the old lord has given Anne-Marie his word, and consequently there is no risk that her family line will not be perpetuated. The word — and that means the family name too — counts for more than a human life.[46]

The inviolable coupling of life and death is elegantly illustrated when Goske and Anne-Marie embrace one another at the end of the tale. Anne-Marie's suffering and death in the rye-field gives life to the son, which is precisely what Adam and his aunt are engaged in up at the manor house. At the very moment of Anne-Marie's death, the son lives, in the rye-field and on the manor. Karen Blixen is here portraying the eternal life-cycle. The reference to "the grand, ceremonial manner in which the old lord would state the common happenings of existence"[47] (in the Danish version it is referred to as "God's master of ceremonies", which is more clear-cut and precise) is only a surface critique; fundamentally he is being proclaimed as the agent of the eternal, joyful and remorseless cycle that constitutes life.

Morten Henriksen's screen adaptation of "Sorrow-Acre" and Gabriel Axel's of "Babette's Feast", both from 1987, are first-class examples of filmed versions of Karen Blixen's tales.

In "The Pearls", set around 1863, the aristocratic is directly confronted with the bourgeois. Jensine grows up in a bourgeois environment, with security and certainty as the mainstay; she has been wrapped up and protected on all sides, but is nevertheless coloured by fear to such an extent that she looks upon fear as part of human nature. She marries aristocratic Alexander, who is like a fish in water when dealing with perilous, inconstant and unforeseeable life — therefore *he* does not know the meaning of fear. Alexander derives much enjoyment from gambling and is quite happy — like Babette — to stake all his money, this being the concrete image of his willingness to risk everything. This sounds "really uncanny to Jensine's ears", as her "debts were an abomination"[48] — but in the tale's wider balance of accounts the uncanny is naturally a plus.

On honeymoon in Norway, Jensine tries to instil fear in her husband by behaving recklessly when they walk in the mountains, but this just makes Alexander delight in his wife; he considers the surprising and unpredictable to be important aspects of female nature, and her behaviour tells him that she is on her way over into his aristocratic world. The symbolism in the wild Norwegian highlands leaves no doubt about the passion with which Jensine must become conversant. The central question in the tale is whether Jensine is too powerfully influenced by her environment to achieve the freedom that Alexander represents. She undergoes a crisis of identity, which reaches a climax when it is apparent that she is possibly pregnant. There is deliverance in this, and it can be interpreted as a sign that she has accepted Alexander's world, but it remains uncertain if her childhood milieu has completely released its grip on her. Thus, at the end, we have Jensine and Alexander watching Jensine's aunt approaching along the street, carrying flowers from Jensine's father's garden: "Each from their window, the husband and wife, looked down into the street."[49] It is left open as to whether Jensine and Alexander go their separate ways, or if they remain husband and wife.

A completely different interpretation of Alexander's role is to be found in *Diana's Revenge – two lines in Isak Dinesen's authorship* (1981) by Marianne Juhl and Bo Hakon Jørgensen, in which he is seen as hampering Jensine in her attempt to break away from her bourgeois milieu: "Alexander is no support to Jensine in this matter."[50] He is shallow and irresponsible and incapable of satisfying Jensine's erotic needs: "When he is unable to feel anxiety or be afraid of anything it is likely that his emotional life too is restricted, so that he can feel neither violent joy nor passionate love."[51] *Diana's Revenge* reasons that Alexander and Jensine end up completely detached from one another. Their marriage means a "human and personal reduction"[52] for Jensine, and thus Alexander is an obstruction to her autonomy – meaning that she has to separate herself from him. Such an interpretation completely disregards the enormous positive importance of the aristocratic culture to the whole of Karen Blixen's canon, and is most evident in the opinion of *Diana's Revenge* that Alexander's fearlessness is synonymous with emotional callousness. On the contrary, Karen Blixen's works see fearlessness as a sure sign that the whole gamut of emotions is preserved by virtue of unfettered and natural fulfilment – fearlessness is a decidedly positive factor. That it is possible to talk of a curtailment of the individual in Jensine's case is because she opens herself up to the impersonal, which is the basis of the aristocratic culture. Should the couple separate, it is not Alexander who is the villain, but exclusively the poisoning of a bourgeois milieu.

In "The Heroine" we are not presented with a woman in the process of development; Heloise is a sum of her parts from the outset, and this cannot be meddled with – inasmuch as she would not hesitate to pay with her life in order to preserve her integrity. Her 'wholeness' is disclosed via two men's different views of her. Lamond, a theologian, lives a secluded, bookish life with scholarship and rational understanding as guiding principles; he is representative of England. To him, Heloise could have been taken straight out of an art gallery; she is the ideal woman, above all worldly concerns. Lamond's counter-image is a German colonel who personifies his country's instinctive vitality – he sees in Heloise a flesh and blood woman, sensuality in person. Heloise enlightens them both about their one-sidedness; she is "an embodiment of ancient France"[53] and thus the ideal and the reality, spirit and body, in perfect harmony.

Heloise is a true aristocrat, which she also demonstrates by embodying the concepts of courage and honour. Following the outbreak of the Franco–Prussian war in 1870, the German colonel holds Lamond, Heloise and other refugees as prisoners in a hotel. He makes Heloise a proposal: she can secure release for herself and the others by coming to him dressed like the goddess Venus. But Heloise would rather lose her life than her honour. Instead of executing them, the colonel releases the prisoners, and he rewards Heloise with roses and a dedication – "To a heroine"[54] – demonstrating that her action has made him see the other side of her, the ideal woman. In other words: there is freedom in Heloise's doubleness. Lamond does not comprehend this doubleness until many years later when he encounters Heloise again in a Parisian music hall, where she has worked as a naked dancer since long before they first met. Lamond and the colonel are not just two individuals, but also the unrealised sides of one another, revealed by virtue of Heloise.

Both Lamond and the colonel harbour strong feelings for Heloise – the tale is also a love story with reference to the famous twelfth-century romance between Abélard and Heloise, which has survived in the *Letters of Abelard and Heloise*. However, Karen Blixen gleaned more comprehensive and direct inspiration from two short stories: the Danish writer Steen Steensen Blicher's "Den sachsiske Bondekrig" (The Saxon Peasant War, 1827) and the German author Jakob Wassermann's *Golowin* (1920). She writes about these stories in a letter from Africa:

"In one of Blicher's stories, the heroine is given the choice between her young brother's life and the sacrifice of her (womanly) honor to the enemy commander, and neither she nor her brother entertain a moment's doubt: – it is his life that must be sacrificed. In a modern story, – by Jakob Wassermann, – a Bolshevik officer gives a young lady the promise of sparing a company of refugees if she will come to his quarters at night; she hesitates no longer than Blicher's brother and sister, but replies: 'Yes, of course, – here I am.' I think there are very few young women whose conscience and moral sense would not bid them give the same answer. For they no longer feel their 'womanliness' to be the most sacred element in their nature, and the concept of 'womanly honor' is of no importance to them, hardly any meaning. – Likewise Blicher's young nobleman would have chosen death rather than hang his escutcheon round the neck of a pig, while I am pretty sure that nowadays no nobleman in the world, – anyway in any of the civilized countries, – would not be prepared to do so with a perfectly good conscience if thereby he could save his friends' lives, or even his own ... " [55]

"The Heroine" is written in the spirit of Blicher as a revolt against the modern perspective, which only functions on the purely particularised level and ignores supra-individual ideals and values. Heloise demonstrates what has been lost: the strength to be drawn from underlying powers. Perhaps as an ironic salute to Wassermann, who lets his characters get off cheaply, there is a small station in "The Heroine" called Wasserbillig (literally: water-cheap).

"Alkmene" is probably the grimmest of all Karen Blixen's tales, relentlessly pursuing the story of how a parsonage milieu crushes the life out of an unspoilt child of nature. The story has, like many others, "Shakespeare's inspirational force"[56] – the source here being the dreadfully maltreated Perdita in *The Winter's Tale*. But the first-person narrator, Vilhelm, who professes neutrality but nonetheless, with his passivity and irresponsibility, is party to the sad fate he recounts, is clearly inspired by Steen Steensen Blicher.

Jens Jespersen ekes a living as a parson in a remote area of Jutland – this being a manifestation of his cowardly abandonment of youthful dreams of becoming a poet, which he now wards off by referring to them as having been an illness. As a young man, he had written an epic entitled "Alkmene", and by abandoning the child Alkmene he repeats the renunciation he made in his youth. The parson marries Gertrud, who is good-natured and cheerful, but her spontaneity is soon subdued at the parsonage – the couple's childlessness speaking for itself. Therefore they adopt Alkmene, who is of ambiguous parentage – but this uncertainty stands in positive contrast to the security in which she is enveloped. Nevertheless, there can be no denying her aristocratic descent – underscored by her sense of well-being when wearing a dress that had belonged to the deceased lady of the manor. Alkmene is by nature fearless and extravagant; this characterisation however, is simply an indication of the enormous resources she has at her disposal. She is heir to a huge fortune that she has known about all her life – this is also an image of the riches she has *inside*. The inheritance is thought to have come from a demonic source and is thus on a par with the lottery winnings in "Babette's Feast", which are called "ungodly affairs" and are Babette's 'capital'.

Out in the countryside, Alkmene and Vilhelm are unfettered and have a deep understanding of one another, but this is suspended the moment they step into the parsonage. Karen Blixen quite likely had a novel she admired in mind: Emily Brontë's *Wuthering Heights* (1847), in which Catherine and the *foundling* Heathcliff are symbiotically in their element in the imposing wild landscape, but are separated and stifled in the civilised interior of Thrushcross Grange. The fact that the parsonage smothers Alkmene is demonstrated in the gradual erosion of her Græcism. The parson and his wife shorten the name Alkmene, from Greek mythology meaning "woman of might", to Mene, which in "The Book of Daniel" means: "God hath numbered thy kingdom, and finished it."[57] In "The Book of Daniel" this is the judgment pronounced on the non-believing Belshazzar, but it is also the writing on the wall for Alkmene! By the time Alkmene reaches the age at which she should be confirmed, the parson completely stops the lessons in Greek mythology that she loved, and the connection is definitively severed.

One by one, Gertrud corrects Alkmene's 'flaws', and the girl becomes acquainted with fear. She is not allowed to have girlfriends, and Gertrud is loath to let her out of her sight; this also applies to the future, as Gertrude declares that, even were it the King's son, she would not allow anyone to marry Alkmene. The execution of a condemned man on the North Common in Copenhagen is a brutal symbol of Gertrud's 'killing' of Alkmene; if the means are formidable enough, a milieu can crush even the strongest individual. In a letter, Karen Blixen describes quite precisely this total envelopment: "for Alkmene there is the sinister aspect to the situation that, whilst all her surroundings are forcing her to go there, they at the same time act as if utterly ignorant of the existence of the Common."[58] The execution is also an image of Alkmene's desire for fatal vengeance on Gertrud. But Gertrud's death sentence has already been implemented, as in relation to Alkmene she has merely repeated the treatment she *herself* was subjected to by the parson. Alkmene has her revenge, however, by taking lifelessness to the point of madness – but therein lies Gertrud's definitive victory: the parson dies, and from then on, moving to an isolated sheep farm, she has Alkmene completely to herself. In addition, Alkmene becomes like a mother to Gertrud, who thus gains her adopted daughter's full attention. Their life on the sheep farm is a biting satire of bourgeois existence. Everything is scrupulously clean, but only the strictly necessary rooms are used; they live extremely frugally and work without rest, with the one objective of putting everything into the savings bank.

Karen Blixen's preoccupation with being lost in or fulfilling dreams is brought into full play in "The Dreaming Child". We are now in Copenhagen in the mid-1800s. Jens spends the first six years of his life in a backyard of a slum neighbourhood; he grows up with his dream-world, which is apparently made real when he is adopted by a 'grand' young couple, Jakob and Emilie Vandamm – who are able to at last realise their dream of having a child. Emilie finds herself in a situation similar to that of Lucie Vandamm in "The Hermits", but the outcome is different. Jakob and Emilie's childlessness is the result of Emilie's unconsummated love for one Charlie Dreyer, which she cannot get over, and therefore she is incapable of giving herself to Jakob. Charlie symbolises Emilie's over-romantic expectations of marriage, but his death is also a representation of how the institution of marriage destroys the romantic – although Jakob and his Madonna-picture of Emilie bears part of the responsibility for their childlessness.

Their adopted son, Jens, dies – a sad event demonstrating what can happen if one abandons oneself to dreams as, despite going to live with Jakob and Emilie, Jens cannot move beyond his dreamworld. His fate is particularised in a metaphor taken from nature: "There are some young trees which, when they are planted have the root twisted, and will never take hold in the soil. They may shoot out a profusion of leaves and flowers, but they must soon die. Such was the way with Jens. He had sent out his small branches upwards and to the sides, had fared excellently of the chameleon's dish and eaten air, promise-crammed, and the while he had forgotten to put out roots."[59] The same image is used in "The Dreamers", where dreams that are not nourished by substance in reality are bluntly called: "the well-mannered people's way of committing suicide."[60]

But, at the same time, Jens tells us something about Jakob and Emilie; he symbolises the ideal notion that keeps Jakob at a distance from Emilie and the dreamworld in which she is close to abandoning herself and her marriage. On this level, Jens *is* a child of Emilie and Charlie, as Emilie acknowledges, but seeing Jens' fate makes Emilie realise the unreality in the dream of lost love for Charlie, just as Jakob sees through fixation on the ideal. On the symbolic level, Jens' death is therefore positive: it shows that the oblivious dreamworld and the unadulterated ideal perish *in* Emilie and Jakob. Jens' death means that Emilie and Jakob find one another, and in so doing the dream of love returns, but now in a realistic form. "The Dreaming Child" thus both challenges abandonment to dreams and is a story about *realising* one's dreams.

Verdict on Conscience

The Angelic Avengers

In 1944 Karen Blixen published *The Angelic Avengers*, her only novel. It was written in Danish, but claimed to be a translation of a French novel written during the inter-war period by Pierre Andrézel. Karen Blixen took this decision on purely practical grounds: during World War II, the German occupying power in Denmark only permitted translations from English if at the same time the publisher translated a book from German, but as the publishing houses lacked resources and had no market for books translated from German, translations from English were ruled out.[61] Karen Blixen wrote *The Angelic Avengers* to amuse herself and to alleviate the sense of imprisonment during the war. But she categorically denied that the novel dealt with the Dano–German conflict, as a number of reviewers maintained. Her claim is also credible as there is nothing in the novel that turns away from the characteristic themes and towards a specific treatment of the period of German occupation. Karen Blixen long and stubbornly denied authorship of *The Angelic Avengers*. She did, however, place clearly on record that it "sails rather close to the borderline of what an author can venture",[62] and she was disappointed that the reviewers preferred it to her earlier works.

In several respects *The Angelic Avengers* is indeed pure melodrama: the improbable, the easy solutions and romantic-fiction love do not always have an underlying depth of symbolism. But, by way of compensation, in pastor Pennhallow we are introduced to one of Karen Blixen's most fascinating characters, whose verdict on conscience is of great significance to Karen Blixen's entire canon of literary works. Two pure and innocent young English girls lead us to the pastor and thus into the darkness of evil.

Lucan and Zosine are children of the Victorian era. When they decide to pretend that they are sisters, they agree to say that there is a six-month age difference between them – such is their 18-year-old ignorance. Their mothers are dead, from lack of love, as marriages of convenience are the order of the day. The girls are strongly attached to their fathers, for whom their principal task is to be an adornment, and they have the prospect of husbands who are new father figures. Older, powerful and affluent men 'buy' young girls. It is taken for granted that the girls sacrifice themselves completely to others and never consider their own needs. This is the environment from which the girls set themselves free by combining their strengths: Lucan's common sense and Zosine's adventurousness. Their union is embodied in them from the outset, as they were born on the same day. The girls proceed to France and the home of Pennhallow, who has himself been banished from England. He has two closely connected sides to his character: he is both that which England cannot accommodate, and which is thus explained away as evil, and all the evil resulting from Victorian renunciation. There is a clear message in his surname: confinement (pen) as a consequence of sanctification (hallow).

Through extensive tuition, Pennhallow equips Lucan and Zosine with something to which English women only later gained access: a knowledge that provides them with great power. We are told that Pennhallow knew the girls better than they knew themselves, but through him they arrive at this understanding of themselves. In other words, he *is* the spirit that has been suppressed in them, but which now comes into its own. In the person of Pennhallow, the girls also encounter the arts, as he both draws and plays the flute. Pennhallow is inflexible dignity and profound joy; he is "something more than a man, a kind of silent, old icon",[63] and thus an eternal force, which time might be able to disguise, but not eradicate. This relates to that evil which is naturally inherent: "For the evil of this world is mighty, an abyss, a deep sea that cannot be emptied with a spoon, or by any human acts or measures"[64] – as Pennhallow says. It cannot but be of benefit to the girls that Pennhallow also gives them full instruction in this aspect of life.

Pennhallow is devoid of conscience, and he thus stops at nothing: "Everything is permitted me."[65] His dignity is also the fortunate consequence of this total lack of boundaries, which is in diametrical opposition to the restrictions and qualms of conscience that the girls have been used to. This is a precise echo of Dostoevsky's *Crime and Punishment* (1866) in which Svidrigaylov, dissolute and totally lacking in conscience, says to the ascetic Raskolnikov: "it seems to me that I am probably five times as healthy as you."[66] With his characterisation of conscience, it is allotted to Pennhallow to excoriate the controlling authorities of the strict moral environments that Karen Blixen often depicts:

> "*Believe me, I know pious people and their consciences . . . Their consciences left them no peace, and permitted them nothing in all the world. It had got stronger and more delicate instruments to torture them with than those that I have handled in the vaults of the old prisons, and in the hands of their conscience they were as naked, pinioned and gagged as the people who were brought down there . . . they had to starve their bodies and souls to death at the bidding of their conscience . . . And their bitter, undying envy of those who were not slaves of their consciences stuck in them, like the poles on which the victims of old days were impaled, and made their souls grow gangrenous round it.*"[67]

Pennhallow illustrates what Lucan and Zosine shut out of their lives, and in this sense he is not a danger to them. On the contrary, via his tuition he wants to gain access to them, and in so doing to act out his other role as the demon spawned of their suppression. Pennhallow is only dangerous when he is held hostage to conscience, for then he threatens to avenge. We are told that "his whole being is mendacity",[68] but emphasis is put on the repression from which the demon is begotten and the falsity of incarceration. In *Crime and Punishment*, Svidrigaylov's hedonism is also a picture of the intensification of Raskolnikov's urges, because he has relegated them to a life of darkness. Svidrigaylov is therefore a danger to Raskolnikov, but when Raskolnikov opens himself up to the world, Svidrigaylov dies. In similar fashion, Pennhallow's unscrupulous perversions are also a manifestation of the over-dimensioning of all things natural to be found in a restrictive community. And he, too, dies as a consequence of compliance: Lucan and Zosine ask for mercy on his behalf, and with this sympathetic gesture they turn the demon out of their lives. Contributory to this process is, moreover, a potent mixture of African and Greek enlightenment in the person of the black woman, Olympia, who appears at the critical moment. Obstacles lying in the path of true love are swept aside, and the novel ends happily with a double wedding.

Childlike Wealth

"The Ghost Horses"

Karen Blixen's tales have, of course, often been the subject of interpretative readings; in 1950, for example, there were radio broadcasts of both Bodil Ipsen reading "Babette's Feast" and Ingeborg Brams reading "The Ghost Horses".[69] "The Ghost Horses" was originally written for an American magazine (*Ladies' Home Journal*), which published it in 1951. It was later published as a book in Denmark in 1955. It is a singular tale, characterised by an elegant simplicity, under which there lies considerable depth.

The central character is a little girl, Nonny; she is six years old, as were Jens in "The Dreaming Child" and Alkmene. Karen Blixen often introduces us to her child characters at that age, when the purely ingenuous stage is over and conflict is generated when children encounter expectations from an adult world that has lost the enriching attachment to the 'childlike', in the best sense of the word. Nonny's playmate, Billy, has died; his death demonstrates the harsh reality that the adult world is fatally opposed to the playful world. Nonny's mother, for instance, is completely unaware of Billy's existence. Billy's death causes Nonny to become ill, and for the first time her mother takes care of her; but the one who is the cause of an illness cannot, of course, cure it. From a medical point of view, Nonny is completely healthy, because science is dryly rational and must consequently regard the loss of imagination as the transition to a normal condition.

Some family jewellery has a completely different value for Nonny than for the adults. Nonny and Billy found the jewellery in an old harness room above the garages that had once been stables, and the jewellery provided precious toys for the children, who transformed the pieces into ghost horses. The adults believe that the jewellery disappeared many years previously when a relation, the young mistress of the house at the time, ran away with her stable boy. What Nonny has right in front of her is, in other words, an item of lost value for her mother, who might wish for the return of the jewellery, but from completely materialistic motives.

The children's ghost horses are in direct contrast to a mechanical

Anders Kopp, son of Karen Blixen's niece,
Anne, listening to the storyteller, *c.*1959
Photograph: Erik Kopp

horse – the modern toy with which the adults try unsuccessfully to distract Nonny. In "On Mottoes of My Life", Karen Blixen makes a comparison between old and modern toys, which goes straight to the essence of "The Ghost Horses":

> *"Children of my day, even in great houses, had very little in the way of toys. Toy shops were almost unknown; modern mechanical playthings, which furnish their own activity, had hardly come into existence. One might, of course, buy oneself a hobbyhorse, but generally speaking an individually selected knotty stick from the woods, upon which imagination might work freely, was dearer to the heart. We were not observers, as children today seem to be from birth, of their own accord; and not utilizers, as they are brought up to be; we were creators. Our knotty stick, for all working purposes, in appearance and as far as actual horsepower went, came nearer to Bucephalus and eight-hoofed Sleipner, or to Pegasus himself, than any magnificently decorated horse from a smart store."* [70]

The mechanical toy is the auxiliary arm of a modern era with a hostility towards imagination and the free exercise of creation that reaches right into the world of children, cutting off the roots of life. In "The Ghost Horses", this violation of childhood is also an image of the technical era's disregard for the true values of life – thus Nonny is protecting herself from becoming "the child of the motor age".[71] At the same time, the child's world is the imaginative past from which the present has removed itself. The critique of the modern era is the same as in *The Revenge of Truth* – but "The Ghost Horses" takes a more meticulous approach.

Nonny is separated from her mother, and her restoration to health is entrusted to Nonny's uncle, Cedric. He is a painter, and "The Ghost Horses" is that *"Portrait of a Child"*[72] which he paints bit by bit as he becomes better acquainted with Nonny's universe. Cedric demonstrates his special credentials for understanding the child by drawing imaginative pictures for her. He creates a mutual connection that rouses Nonny to acquaint him with what she shared with Billy. In the children's ability to create a unique universe out of old jewellery, Cedric encounters the true essence of art, which is subjugated under the yoke of a modern mentality that relates to reality as if to a prefabricated mechanical toy. Cedric realises the impoverishment of mere observation and reproduction of reality, by means of which art becomes sheer technique.

With Cedric, Nonny progresses to the point that she anticipates her approaching reunion with Billy. Thus there is hope that Nonny will grow up with her imagination intact, but the outcome could also be reunion in death, which indicates both Nonny's uncompromising perspective and the end of imagination.

In E. T. A. Hoffmann's tale "Das fremde Kind" (The Strange Child, 1817) the children Christlieb and Felix are in similar circumstances as Nonny, but in their case the ending is unambiguously happy. The children, who are brother and sister, have the forest as their wonderful fairy-tale playground. They are given some modern toys, but these only keep them away from the forest for a little while, and when they go back the new toys are destroyed *by* the forest. They meet an ally in the forest in the figure of the 'strange' child who is a boy and a girl at the same time and therefore both prince and princess in the realms of childhood and imagination; the strange child is a counterpart to Billy. Christlieb and Felix, however, have an adversary in their teacher, Magister Tinte, who personifies unadulterated, over-refined common sense and is a bitter enemy of play and nature. The strange child, and not Magister Tinte, wins the battle over them, because in this instance the parents are capable of relating to the children's situation and thus ensure that the strange child will live within them to the end of their days.

Origin and Ambiguity

Last Tales

Karen Blixen worked for many years on the novel *Albondocani*, who as mentioned was originally one of the unpredictable ruler Haroun al Raschid's assumed names. Haroun al Raschid was Caliph in Baghdad and thus one of Muhammad's successors as spiritual and political leader. Haroun al Raschid appears in *Thousand and One Nights*, the character Karen Blixen aspired to in her novel. *Albondocani* was also intended to be in the style of Jules Romain's *Les Hommes de Bonne Volonté* (1932–46), a novel in 27 volumes. *Albondocani* was to be 600–900 pages long, have 100 characters and consist of approximately 115 stories, which, as in a cyclical novel, would be self-contained, but also interwoven.[73] Not surprisingly she called it "a giant book"[74] and characterised it as "my fantastic novel".[75] Work on the book, however, progressed slowly, one reason being that she was also working on other collections: *Anecdotes of Destiny, New Gothic Tales* and *New Winter's Tales*. Frustrated by jumping from the one project to the other, she found a solution by collecting the finished tales for *Albondocani*, *New Gothic Tales* and *New Winter's Tales* in a single volume entitled *Last Tales*, which was published in 1957.[76] She had not at that point abandoned her intention of completing *Albondocani*, but apart from the seven tales included in *Last Tales*, she later only wrote one more chapter of the novel, this being the tale "Second Meeting" (1961).[77]

In the *New Winter's Tales* section of *Last Tales*, a story entitled "A Country Tale" provides the best example of Karen Blixen's ability to write in a distinctly exciting manner. The story is about a young landowner, Eitel, who bears the guilt that his father, who died before Eitel was born, had once ordered a peasant, Linnert, to be tied to a timber-mare in the sun, where he died. Eitel's affiliation to his family line is further complicated when his former wet nurse, who is Linnert's daughter, tells him that he is actually her son. She alleges that she changed the master's baby for her own. The tale speaks subtly and without clarification both for and against the nurse's claim. The dubious aspect of her assertion also causes Eitel to question what actually happened between his father and Linnert – because it was the nurse who told him that story in the first place.

The responsibility for his father's action – which cannot be verified – and the sudden doubt about his affiliation to his family – master or peasant – turns Eitel's reality upside down and makes for an ambiguity that permeates the tale and raises many interesting questions. Family, social status, identity and perceptions of reality itself are the issues at stake.

Eitel has – like many of Karen Blixen's characters – lost his parents, and he is left in doubt about their identity. Furthermore, he has fathered a child who will grow up in the belief that someone else is her father, as the child's mother is a married woman whose husband believes himself to be the father. And the nurse has cast off her son, who must live his life without parents, only to learn that perhaps they are not the people he thought they were anyway. Doubt about parentage, as a symbol of emptiness and ambiguity of an existential, identity or social nature, is an age-old theme. Karen Blixen could have found inspiration as far back as the *Odyssey*, where Telemachus, searching for his father, says: "My mother says that I am his child; but I know not, for never yet did any man of himself know his own parentage."[78] Yes, even the gods can have doubts, as the goddess Eidothea shows when she says of the sea god Proteus: "He, they say, is my father that begat me."[79] In "A Country Tale" there is mention of Orestes, who kills his stepfather and his mother, thus avenging their murder of his father, Agamemnon. Orestes is a predecessor of Hamlet, who is subject to the same loss of a father and ensuing dilemma with a stepfather. Later on, in Henrik Ibsen's *The Wild Duck* (1884), the central character, whilst still believing in his status as father, is spoken of thus: "And there he sits, childlike and trusting, caught in this web of deceit – sharing his roof with a woman like that, never suspecting that what he calls his home is built upon a lie!"[80] This leads naturally to Johan August Strindberg's *The Father* (1887), in which there is a scene where the Captain descends from the loft carrying a pile of books all dealing with doubt about paternity – the *Odyssey* being on the top of the pile. Perhaps Karen Blixen was acknowledging inspiration from Strindberg in Eitel's other names, which are Johan August. In James Joyce's novel *Ulysses* (1922), which shares original Greek sources with Karen Blixen's works and similarly engages the eternal themes, the lack of a father is summed up: "if the father who has not a son be not a father can the son who has not a father be a son?"[81]

Before the nurse tells Eitel that he is her son, he says: "I shall not, at the moment when I have become, truthfully, what I am, in cutting off my roots, turn myself into a shadow, into nothingness."[82] But this is exactly what happens, and in the description of the ambiguity in which he is subsequently embroiled Karen Blixen takes up the threads of her predecessors in an impeccable manner.

Among the other themes in "A Country Tale" is the same relationship between nobility and peasant that we found in "Sorrow-Acre" – Eitel and the nurse's son are thus closely united in the entanglement. And at the same time, the nurse's son – who is a murderer and a wild animal – is another side of Eitel with which he has to come to terms, just as Lise is reconciled with the sheep thief in "The Ring".

A Preliminary Look at

Anecdotes of Destiny

Anecdotes of Destiny, to be considered in detail below, evolved at the end of the 1940s. It was originally Karen Blixen's label for stories she wrote in order to earn money and thus have better working conditions for "my 'real' writings".[83]

But gradually, as she honed the collection, she stopped judging the stories as second-rate. Many stories were considered along the way, but the five stories making up the final version from 1958 had almost been settled by 1953 – she was just a little unsure as to whether or not "Tempests" should be included. In 1953 her plan had been that *Anecdotes of Destiny* should be the fourth section of *Last Tales*, but the stories ended up in two collections, which she wanted to be published on the same day. This idea, however, ran into difficulties from the publisher's side, and Karen Blixen chose to publish *Last Tales* first because she attributed it greater significance in her body of work, and, having been absent for many years, she wanted to return to the public stage at full strength. But she saw no difference in the literary quality of the two books; *Anecdotes of Destiny* was simply composed for different kinds of instruments, playing a lighter note.[84]

Art and Reality

Ehrengard

Ehrengard is one of the tales Karen Blixen had in mind for *Anecdotes of Destiny*, but which she left out as she was not satisfied with it. It was originally written in 1952, but was reworked twice, the final revision being in 1962; it was published as an independent book in 1963. In *Ehrengard* two principalities are on the verge of collapse because the prince of one is only interested in spiritual and artistic matters, whereas the princess of the other represents a lineage that *is* the unconscious course of life. With usual Blixenesque logic, both principalities are saved when the prince and princess marry one another. The central character is, however, Ehrengard, who becomes the princess's chaperon. She has had – just like Athena and Calypso in *Seven Gothic Tales* – such a strict moral upbringing that she considers this morality to be a law of nature. But Ehrengard's ignorance is also a manifestation of an 'untouched' state that makes her pure, pre-conscious nature. She has never before paused for reflection when she meets the artist Cazotte, the man who has been detailed to awaken her consciousness. But *Ehrengard* is not least a tale about the relationship between art and the material of reality; in Ehrengard, Cazotte finds an unworked "block of marble".[85] Cazotte believes that he can beguile and control his material – Ehrengard – through and through, but he discovers to his cost that the material has its unpredictability, of which the artist must be accepting. Cazotte wants to force Ehrengard's inmost substance from her and display it in perfect clarity, but *he* is forced to take into account a "void",[86] which is apparent in the surprises by means of which *she* at the same time beguiles *him*. If the artist endeavours to be in total command of his material and thereby elevate art above reality, he offends against that very reality which also has its unpredictability. Reality has laws to which art must defer; conversely, reality first comes into existence in the artist's interpretation. This is precisely the relationship generated between Ehrengard and Cazotte. In beginning to lead Ehrengard, Cazotte is also controlled by her. The fertility of this dialectic becomes apparent in the child of the prince and princess, which is also said to be Cazotte and Ehrengard's child. But both cases signify a union between spirit and nature, art and reality.

Love and Ideals

Essays

Besides the essays in *Shadows on the Grass* and in *Karen Blixen's Drawings*, over the years Karen Blixen wrote a series of other essays that are found in *Samlede essays* (*Collected Essays*, 1985).[87] The book is printed using the modern orthography, even though in the essay "On Orthography" (1938) Karen Blixen defends the use of the old orthography, which was indeed used in the earlier, but not quite so comprehensive collection, *Essays* (Essays, 1965).

Three of the essays – "On Modern Marriage and Other Observations" (1924), "Daguerreotypes" (1951) and "Oration at a Bonfire, Fourteen Years Late" (1952) – discuss the relationship between the sexes, in general or in love and marriage. In "On Modern Marriage and Other Observations" Karen Blixen maintains that the old institution of marriage has outlived itself because the ideals that sustained it are now empty shells. It is a question of consistently crushing the shells, so that no one is imprisoned in a room where "the air is stale".[88] In this situation she sees two possibilities: either a new marriage should be built up on different, viable ideals – of which she names consideration of 'blood' as being central – or one must put free love into practice. Both forms can exist, side by side, as options for the individual. Free love should *not* be understood in the unrestrained sense of our times, for Karen Blixen emphatically insisted on fidelity for as long as a relationship lasted, but it is a matter of keeping love clear of all the restrictions that dissipate it.

Free love is found where ideal love alone reigns supreme. A high ideal of free love is the prerequisite for being able to practise it, and Karen Blixen would like to see this on such a scale that "love is openly acknowledged as an ideal".[89] In so doing, it would finally be possible to illuminate an area that has been "completely neglected".[90] Karen Blixen looks with aristocratic optimism upon the possibility of this coming about, as she is of the firm conviction that no ideal can be too noble: "In the long run there is no effort, danger or suffering that can stop humanity striving to achieve an ideal . . . "[91]

The essay "H. C. Branner: *The Riding Master*" (1949), which Karen Blixen calls a review, reveals a penetrating literary critic whose detailed commentary on Branner's novel expresses attitudes that – as we shall see – are also relevant to her own works. Branner himself considered the essay to be an outstanding analysis of his novel, uncovering layers of which he had not been aware.[92]

In "On Mottoes of My Life" (1959) Karen Blixen describes the strength that a motto can generate, and then proceeds to list the mottoes that have strengthened her personally – leading to discussion of central phases and events in her life. A report she read in the newspaper, about a French boat that had gone down near Iceland with her flag flying, had great significance for Karen Blixen. The boat had been named "Pourquoi pas?" – "Why not?" – and in this she saw "a directive, a call of wild hope". "Pourquoi pas?" became the motto for an entire oeuvre: "Under this sign – at times very doubtful about the whole thing, but still, as it were, in the hands of an exacting and joyful spirit – I finished my first book. And this third motto of mine may be said to stand over all my books."[93]

Dialogue and Responsibility

Karen Blixen in Denmark: Letters, 1931–1962

Karen Blixen in Denmark: Letters, 1931–62 was published in 1996 and is a very comprehensive and essential documentation of Karen Blixen's life from the time of her return home from Africa until her death in 1962. Unlike its predecessor, *Letters from Africa, 1914–1931*, the new collection also includes letters *to* Karen Blixen, presented with her own letters in a fascinating dialogue form.

The letters give an impression of day-to-day life at Rungstedlund and an insight into relationships with family and friends. The 'intimate sphere', however, provides a concrete picture of Karen Blixen's attitude as regards the Danish mentality in general, which is in turn inextricably bound up with problems of coming to terms with European life. In another vein, there are letters mourning the loss of her farm and life in Africa, observing developments in Kenya and following the prospects for the indigenous peoples with concern – but here Europe is also held responsible.

This collection of letters is a new and crucial contribution to an understanding of Karen Blixen's writings. It is intriguing to follow the genesis of her work and read her own assessment of it. We are also presented with other authors' sometimes detailed interpretations of the works and Karen Blixen's response, and also her opinion of reactions from readers and reviewers. The letters also paint a picture of Karen Blixen's views on the works of other authors, and about the development of literature and the various literary trends and genres. There are reflections on the mission of art and its social significance and, of course, discussions about the fundamental questions of the job, such as artistic inspiration and the prerequisites of creativity.

Specific political and historical circumstances are considered; religious, philosophical and existential questions are debated at greater length. There are observations of notable import, often with an unambiguous message. The opinions expressed have an unequivocal perspective, such as, for example, the recurring view that one "cannot 'be let off cheaply' . . . it is worth paying whatever it costs".[94]

PART II

When Destiny Comes Calling

Prelude

Karen Blixen's concept of destiny is divided into the destiny common to all and that which bears upon the individual; but in order for the individual to be able to draw on all particularised aptitudes and thereby realise personal destiny in full, the individual must deal openly with and incorporate all aspects of the common destiny. The destiny shared by all is that of being placed in a life which spans divine and demonic forces – these being both active in the external world and as innate human potential. It is as potential that destiny volunteers its services, because it is up to the individual in action to choose both the divine and the demonic sides of life. This is the prerequisite of the next choice: the decision to realise particularised aptitudes and talents. Optimal conditions are provided by growing up in a milieu and a culture which are receptive to all the forces in life; on the other hand, it can be considerably more problematic if one has grown up in a milieu and a culture based on opting out of one of the sides of life. In other words, one can be in a more or less momentous situation, but liberation and accomplishment depend on the courage and determination exercised by the individual. The forces that Karen Blixen's characters have for or against them can also be manifested in specific individuals who exercise a power over others, which, in a positive example, builds on both the divine and the demonic and, in a negative example, on exclusion of one of the sides. Thus someone who has grown up with optimal conditions will have their fate put to the test in an encounter with a negative agent of power, and conversely someone who has been stifled by their milieu will have the potential for liberation in an encounter with a positive agent of power. Tragedy occurs when the qualities of character needed either to withstand or to challenge are absent; the stifling elements in a milieu can also be so extreme that the character *is* annihilated, as demonstrated in "Alkmene". It is typical of Karen Blixen's characters that they can fulfil themselves in love and as artists – where the issue of art also concerns realising true art.[1] In *Anecdotes of Destiny* the theme of destiny is played through in the variations outlined above. But it is true to say that many of Karen Blixen's other tales could be called, with just as much justification, anecdotes of destiny.

I The Aristocratic Art

The twofold nature of the tale

In the first tale in the collection, "The Diver", which was originally published in 1954,[2] Saufe moves from the sky to the sea, these being other words for the divine and the demonic. First he plans to construct wings in order to get up into the consummate light and thus into a state of blessed calm and serenity. By so doing, he shrouds himself in that sphere in which Martine and Philippa in "Babette's Feast" live their entire lives, and the first part of "The Diver" is also a story about the cost of a purely 'heavenly' life. Saufe's preoccupation with angels blinds him to the real world. A minister to the King says that Saufe is dangerous because he dreams great dreams, but is easy to handle because he lacks knowledge of the real world in which dreams are tested. It is not that there is anything wrong in the dreams themselves, but in their lack of connection with reality – if there was a connection Saufe could fulfil himself, but the minister sees a danger that he will lose himself. Therefore the minister and the authorities he represents furnish Saufe with a combination of dream and reality in the form of Thusmu, a young dancing girl, who is both utterly worldly and also angelic. But Saufe never detects this twofold nature. At first he only sees the angel in her, thereby revealing the self-delusion that is a consequence of his one-sidedness. This is followed by a process in which the discovery of eroticism in his relationship with Thusmu takes him away from his work with the wings, which end up being eaten by rats. But this is merely a manifestation of his original one-sidedness being replaced by another. Eventually, he can only see the worldly aspect in Thusmu and thus excludes the hope – the spiritual – that she entreats him also to see in her dancing. Saufe himself says that he has become an enemy to the angels and thereby an enemy to God and "whoever is an enemy to God has no hope left. I have no hope, and without hope you cannot fly" (p. 11).[3] This leads to a roaming existence for Saufe, who ends up in the sea. The last part of "The Diver" describes the cost of a life spent among the fish, with no connection to the divine. The sea is the dark and directionless element, but total immersion in it also results in the loss of the 'hands' with which to sow and reap – in other words, without 'hands' there is no potential for constructing anything and thus no prospects in life, as defined by man. Saufe points out that no expectations miscarry in his life as a fish, but this is only because he does not put anything at risk. Completely disillusioned and dispirited as he is, there is no light and no hope ahead.

Saufe does not bring light and dark to the interplay applied by the narrator Mira Jama to his art. The purpose of Mira Jama's storytelling is not simply a judgment on Saufe's twofold one-sidedness, but also – as a kind of prologue – a description of the interplay by means of which *Anecdotes of Destiny* is constructed:

> *"if you follow the career of a single pearl it will give you material for a hundred tales. And pearls are like poets' tales: disease turned into loveliness, at the same time transparent and opaque, secrets of the depths brought to light to please young women, who will recognize in them the deeper secrets of their own bosoms."* (p. 12)

Mira Jama is not afraid of lacking material for his tales, as even a single life is an inexhaustible reservoir, but the profusion of stories which he sees in a unique instance can also be the 'big picture in the detail' or, in other words, the profusion of general material that can be represented by specifics. Mira Jama goes further, with an idea of transformation which is enormously elastic, but the following considerations can lie concealed in it: when a writer converts personal or the bitter experiences of others into art, the experiences are instilled with the beauty which constitutes a work of literature, irrespective of how tragic the events that unfold – put into a story the tragedy develops in grandeur and in so doing also reveals the splendour of fiction. The tragedy is amplified and laid bare in the wider context of the story, by means of which a liberating light is cast upon it. The tale is a source of revelation and thus liberation, where not just the storyteller but also the reader is transformed: Mira Jama says that he "began to tell tales to delight the world" (p. 12). Tales unravel repressions: they bring secrets from the depths into the light.

But the secret aspect also has another significance in which the secret is preserved; this is implied by Mira Jama's call for works of fiction that are both luminously clear and opaque – in other words, both divine and demonic. In this we have the twofold nature that puts Saufe's one-sidedness in its place. As life builds upon both divine and demonic powers, then so must art – it is only by reflecting both sides that true art can be realised and the artist can be fulfilled. The tale must have a level of luminous unambiguity and clarification on which the meaningful dimension in life is played, for "without hope one cannot tell a story" (not in the English language version), and it is therein that the opaque or secret has to be blended to ensure that the universe does not become static, but is kept open to interpretation.

The demonic is also the inevitable suffering which the work of art must incorporate; it must re-create "a sublime world, with all things necessary to the purpose in it, and none left out", as described in "The Cardinal's First Tale".[4] Consummation and tribulation, joy and sorrow must be blended in the work of art, as in the synthesis there is greatness in suffering and death, and the divine steps into character as worldly delight.

A tale does not exist without its dark side where the devil plays his hand; one cannot play "with a pack of cards in which even the ace of spades is pink", as the painter says in Karen Blixen's tale "Carnival".[5] In *Karen Blixen in Denmark: Letters, 1931–62* she writes about the special impression which a painting by Degas made on her: "I remember a painting by Degas . . . it was one big declaration of how glorious, deep, divinely *black* – the colour black, – is. It has been of great joy and comfort to me in life."[6] Karen Blixen attributes the same declaration to the painter in "Carnival" when developing his theory of colour:

> "*I know that there is, somewhere, a theory that black will make your coloring heavy. It is a very great mistake. On the contrary, it makes for lightness and does away with greasiness, which is the most deadly danger to a painter. The clay, as you know, before the baking is also greasy, soft, and heavy, but in the burning pottery becomes black, and grows at the same time hard, dry, and light. Thus life. It is necessary to get black into it somehow. You young people know of no black, and what is the result? Alas, that your existence becomes every day more flat and greasy.*"[7]

In "Babette's Feast", Babette, via her art, unites the divine and the demonic and she introduces the colour black into a very flat and greasy environment. This union, which is anticipated in "The Diver", is a manifestation of an aristocratic art that is not just the ideal in *Anecdotes of Destiny*, but in Karen Blixen's entire canon. As is evident from the above, the theme of art plays a role throughout all her work. In the following section other perspectives on the aristocratic art will be examined, by means of which we shall be able to define and broaden the concept.

Silence and statement

In Laurence Sterne's novel *Tristram Shandy* (1760–7) numerous passages consist of just dashes or stars, by means of which the reader can imagine the content of these gaps in the text. At one point there are two completely blank pages, allowing the readers to compose their own portrait of one of the female characters, and elsewhere two pages are quite simply completely black. In "Master Tailor Synaal's Tale" Johannes Ewald vies with Sterne; the body of the tale claims to be Synaal's own written account of his life, whole pages of which are illegible because they have either had ink spilled all over them or have been used as wrapping for half a pound of butter that Synaal has hidden from his wife. The reader is invited to fill in the missing passages, and this invitation is also found in Hans Christian Andersen's travel book *Fodreise fra Holmens Kanal til Østpynten af Amager* (*Walking Tour from Holmen's Canal to the Eastern Point of Amager*, 1829), which has a truly open ending as the final – the fourteenth – chapter consists of blank pages; the ending is a blank rather than the unlucky number thirteen "in order that one of the chapters should not die".[8]

The old storyteller in Karen Blixen's meta-story "The Blank Page" would seem to have a whole tradition behind her when she says: "Where the storyteller is loyal, eternally and unswervingly loyal to the story, there, in the end, silence will speak ... And where does one read a deeper tale than upon the most perfectly printed page of the most precious book? Upon the blank page."[9] Silence and the blank page are the optimum statement! The white sheet of paper is both luminously clear and receptive of new stories; the true conclusion consists of blank pages. When every conclusion is thus a beginning, we have the never-ending or immortal story, because silence and the blank page are the ultimate uninterpretability. At the same time, silence is the one explanation to which there is no retort. Karen Blixen's meta-story is so constructed that the explanations can continue for all eternity. The never-ending story can therefore also be read as a combination of a tale of period-specific and eternal themes in which the latter ought to form the central plane. That "the very first germ of a story will come from some mystical place outside the story itself"[10] is indicative of these eternal themes, which are universal destiny and the immortal myths through which it is often conveyed.

What ought to apply to the story, ought also apply to the characters in the story. In the essay "Til fire Kultegninger" (Of Four Charcoal Drawings), in which Karen Blixen writes about her own drawings and paintings, she makes the following comment about a young girl who sat for her drawing *Ung pige med højhalset bluse* (*Young girl with high-necked blouse*): "I remember that the young girl captivated me by something graceful, as if altogether impassive, like a blank sheet of paper."[11] Grace consists of impassivity and that which is unwritten. What she says about the model also applies to the characters in Karen Blixen's stories. The open face again shows the twofold nature of serenity and the indefinable – everything can be read into it. At the same time, impassivity implies the absence of individual features. And as the characters no longer express individuality, silence steps in and thus the eternal nature speaks in them. In "The Cardinal's First Tale", the Cardinal says on Karen Blixen's behalf: "You will see the characters of the true story clearly, as if luminous and on a higher plane, and at the same time they may look not quite human . . . Whatever he is in himself, the immortal story immortalizes its hero."[12] The story does not take the individuality of a person into consideration, because it wants to bring out the universal, supra-individual through its characters and thereby make them the bearers of the immortal, mythical material. An 'enlargement' of the characters then occurs, illustrated on several occasions in Karen Blixen's works by portraits of characters who shrink and become lifeless, having cast giant-sized, vigorous shadows on the wall. In her essay "H. C. Branner: *The Riding Master*", Karen Blixen writes about the eradication of individual features in the main character of *The Riding Master* in his assumption of a mythological status: "the mythical figure enlarges him tremendously, gives him life of its life and blood of its blood. And makes him inhuman."[13] The same 'making inhuman' of characters is found in Karen Blixen's stories.

The artist and freedom

The prerequisite for creating this aristocratic art is that the artist disengages from the private sphere, for it is only in this way that universality can be expressed through the artistic person. The true artist is "the man who has no existence of his own – because the existence of each human being is his".[14] Like the aristocrat in "Sorrow-Acre", who makes sure his family line continues by setting himself aside, the artist immortalises the story by suspending personal time-specific issues to make room for eternal themes. Silence is thus given voice. If the artist is liberated, he can give a profound account of the time-specific and private issues which the stories do not attempt to avoid, but penetrate in order to signify that which they obstruct: the freedom that lies in the union of the eternally divine and demonic forces.

Life-giving narrative

Immortal stories fulfil an eternal need: "Stories have been told as long as speech has existed, and *sans* stories the human race would have perished, as it would have perished *sans* water."[15] So says the Cardinal in "The Cardinal's First Tale". His fear is that the aristocratic art is on the wane, and therefore the human race is withering spiritually. In "Babette's Feast", Babette realises aristocratic art for an 'audience' that understands nothing about it. One of the tragedies of the story is that there is no longer an audience that is capable of comprehending it.

The Cardinal sees a "new art of narration"[16] surfacing at the expense of the aristocratic. This new art of narration is only concerned with the personal in human nature and current issues, and totally disregards the universal and eternal forces in life. As immortal material disappears from the story, the story itself dies and what is left is a worthless narrative form. The new narrative form is one-dimensional, only passing on what anyone can observe in the immediate reality presented, thereby losing the underlying and enlarging forces which facilitate clarification and penetration. The new narrative form is a sentimental affair that does not have the genuine story's force of cogency and thus is no longer a question of art. When one has "become too familiar with life" one loses the breadth of view and possibility to see "that one thing is much worse than the other", as the narrator Mira Jama says in "The Dreamers".[17] This statement about vulgarisation and standardisation is underpinned by a very concrete metaphor for the new narrative form in "The Deluge at Norderney": "The young men of our days, who wear tight trousers which oblige them to keep two valets for drawing them on . . . may be more human, but surely they have nothing divine. They may have the facts of life on their side, while the legs of the women, under their petticoats, are ideas."[18] As defined in Karen Blixen's works, this new narrative form could best be translated as pure realism and indeed even social realism, but overall this also implies a distinction between bourgeois and aristocratic art.

By elevating the aristocratic art and attacking the new narrative form, Karen Blixen's stories naturally speak for themselves. But in the essay "H. C. Branner: *The Riding Master*" she speaks out directly:

"The average Danish reader who, for more than three-quarters of a century has been satiated by the depiction of reality, has, – like the thirsty hart in a dry land that smells and senses a running spring far away –

suspected and sensed myth and adventure far away in The Riding Master
*— the spring, the fountain, the well; and has run towards them . . . Danish
poets of the year of Our Lord 1949! Press the grape of myth or adventure
into the empty goblet of the thirsting people! Do not give them bread when
they ask for stones — a rune stone or the old black stone from the Kaaba;
don't give them a fish, or five small fish, or anything in the sign of the fish,
when they ask for a serpent.* "[19]

The whole of Karen Blixen's canon is an endeavour to quench this thirst,
but at the time she was writing the essay about H. C. Branner, she was
also working on "Babette's Feast". In this story, Babette the artist is akin
to the black stone from the Kaaba in Mecca, and Babette brings stones
and serpents to a community that lives from bread and dried cod.

Fidelity to the artistic nature

In "Babette's Feast", which comes after "The Diver", a fully-developed
and celebrated artist enters an environment that presents the most inaus-
picious conditions for the ongoing fulfilment of art. "Babette's Feast" is
followed by the tale "Tempests", in which nature and nurture have
equipped the young girl Malli with every potential to develop as an
artist. We meet her as she is becoming conscious of all the possibilities
open to her and is at the same time drawn into a bourgeois milieu with
its offer of marriage. In the person of the actor Soerensen she sees a clear
picture of the demands of art, whereas a stay in the Hosewinckel family
home instructs her about the bourgeois way of life. Malli, who wants to
be faithful to her artistic nature, realises that there can be no compro-
mise, her choice must be either/or.

Malli's artistic nature is underlined quite simply in the statement that
she *is* a song. Her father, the sea captain Ross, embodies all the qualities
with which she was born. He is at one with the sea and leaves his wife
and child in order to return to his element; this is the pure spontaneity
that Malli fuses with conscious action. The father provokes unrest in the
bourgeoisie, not least by the uncertainty about where he comes from and
where he later goes to. Malli is therefore of hazy origin, and the mysterious and unaccountable is part of her nature. When Malli, like a true
sailor, saves a ship from being wrecked in a storm, she demonstrates her
great courage and her "unconquerable spirit" (p. 91), but her action also
emphasises her artistic nature as her intrepidity stems from her belief

that she is in a scene from Shakespeare's play *The Tempest* (1611). Malli has always "known in her heart that she would be an actress" (p. 78), the awareness of which comes to her when she sees Soerensen's theatre company in performance; she recognises her destiny with "perfect clarity" (p. 84), and, in her determination to fulfil it, Malli visits Soerensen.

Soerensen personifies the ideal art. He is on the alert and a very matter-of-fact and logical business-like person, at the same time full of "capering, roaring and fantastic grimacing" (p. 72); in other words, he combines soberly calculated and unexpected and surprising behaviour and is thus profitably in tune with nature. His art is rendered of eternal substance as "the immortal minds were his brethren" (p. 73), and he is "the highly appreciated ambassador to the great powers" (p. 72); therefore his pupil Malli is spoken of as being "at the summons of higher powers" (p. 91), which explains why one of their meetings takes place pantomimically: in the silence by means of which these immortal forces speak within them. When Soerensen asks Malli to play Ariel in *The Tempest*, he urges her to forget herself for Shakespeare's sake, and this is a requirement of that dehumanisation which is necessary for her to be able to express the true art which Soerensen sees realised in *The Tempest*. At the same time, by playing the part of the air spirit Ariel, Malli – who is at one with the sea – comes into possession of the celestial perspective and thus comprises the same twofoldness as Soerensen. Therein lies the boundless scope: "Herr Soerensen himself delighted in his freedom; his being blossomed" (pp. 71–2), and in so doing Soerensen is able to create and is entitled to exercise power: "he was a man of a mighty, independent character, which demanded the creation and control of his own world around him" (p. 71). Soerensen is thrilled to have 'created' Malli and calls her his daughter; he is the artistic father figure, and she is right to follow him. But in so doing, Malli, who has always held the town's bourgeoisie in contempt, finds herself in serious conflict with it: "To the townsfolk the life and calling of an actress was something utterly foreign and in itself dubious. Also Malli's special position caused her to be harshly judged or ridiculed" (p. 84). The town's bourgeoisie reacts to this outsider by admitting Malli to its best house, setting off a process that can smother her artistic nature.

When Malli enters the house, she is described in the same way as Babette when she arrives at the rural deanery: "She had entered it pale and dirty of face and in ugly clothes" (p. 98). Fru Hosewinckel explains away Malli's strangeness by likening her to ghosts, whereas Martine and

Philippa see Babette's exertions as the work of the devil. The difference in degree is due to the fact that oppression is extreme in the deanery, yet there are striking similarities with the Hosewinckel home. As opposed to Malli's dirtiness, the Hosewinckels have their "lace curtains" (p. 98). They are God-fearing and rigorously decorous people, whose seclusion from the outside world has made many incapable of living life: "In the family many had died young and unmarried, as if they had been too good and fine to mingle the world's nature with their own" (p. 101). Whereas Soerensen mingles by virtue of his double nature, the Hosewinckel family is based on exclusion and defence. They put "strict border lines" (p. 129) between good and evil and between past and present, and they weigh up life so prudently that emotion and the fantastic are kept out of it. However, Malli's presence in the house means that old Jochum Hosewinckel opens himself to the fantastic and unpredictable and thereby becomes a child again – with no sense of time, indulging his imagination and free of guilt. But Fru Hosewinckel remains firmly resolved to rein Malli in, which could also be due to her alarm at the change in her husband. She regards Malli as "a precious possession" (p. 123) and counters her outburst of independence with the paralysing restrictions of confinement to the home: "Now there must be an end to parties and gatherings, and Malli must remain unobserved and undisturbed under the protection of the house" (p. 124).

The stately house shuts its doors behind the 19-year-old Malli, and she is given the room that used to belong to the shipowner's sister, Sofie, who had died at the age of 19. Youth and vitality are heading for a fall, even though Malli's love for the shipowner's son, Arndt, would seem to herald the opposite. We might very well learn, romantically, that "Arndt's arms would catch her and bear her" (p. 114), but the loss of independence that is also hereby implied becomes extremely clear a moment later as the prisoner symbolism is expanded: "And she was the maid of Arendal who would not consent to be anybody's prize!" (p. 115). Nor have they been engaged for very long before Arndt has to go on a trip for a few days and Malli gets a bit of space – "she almost felt that she needed to draw her breath" (p. 117). To Fru Hosewinckel, marriage between Malli and Arndt is the future; to Malli it means that the 'secret' aspect of her nature will disappear. With a Blicheresque sense for secretiveness as a guiding principle in matters of love,[20] it is stated in "Tempests" that desire is delightful as long as it is secret. But, for marriages contracted in the Hosewinckel house, the secret died. Thus the ruthless consequence of Malli's inclusion in the household is that Ferdinand dies; his natural

Karen Blixen: Still life with bouquet of roses and a book
Oil on canvas, 40.5 × 35.5 cm, c.1916, private collection
Photograph: Ole Woldbye

Karen Blixen: Sketch of a backyard in Copenhagen
Pencil and watercolour on paper, 48 × 29 cm, *c.*1903,
The Karen Blixen Museum
Photograph: Bruun Rasmussen Auctioneers of Fine Arts

realm matches the one Malli comes from, and his death symbolises that which Malli loses in the company of the Hosewinckels. Malli is therefore driven to desperation and grieves deeply over Ferdinand's death, an event that leads her to break loose and seek out Soerensen once more. He has been waiting for Malli's choice, which he knows is a case of either/or, as he is aware that she will be lost to the theatre company if she stays with the Hosewinckels. Like a latter-day Shakespeare, Soerensen also expresses this in his thought that "the house could do with a Fool" (not in the English-language version), highlighting the one-dimensionality that makes it impossible for Malli to preserve her artistic nature in the Hosewinckel household.

It is in Soerensen's troupe, and thus as part of the art for which he stands, that Malli can realise herself as an actor. Their reunion happens just in time, with her clinging to him "like a drowning person to a piece of timber" (p. 136). But she has also reached that Kierkegaardesque despair in which one can distinguish clearly between the essential and non-essential and on that basis make crucial choices. In a farewell letter to Arndt, Malli expresses her regret about her infidelity, but adds: "I carry my unfaithfulness toward you within myself" (p. 146), wherewith she declares that she has chosen to be true to her artistic nature. Malli's father followed his nature and left his wife; Malli also shares this betrayal with Soerensen, who sacrificed marriage, love and "a beautiful little home . . . with curtains and a carpet" (p. 140) for the sake of art. In Soerensen, Malli has found someone "under the same sentence as herself" (p. 140): to be an artist is incompatible with one-dimensional bourgeois life. Echoing Fru Hosewinckel, Soerensen calls Malli "his precious possession" (p. 141), but by virtue of his twofold nature *he* can get Malli to obey the command that she should follow him; Soerensen personifies the art by which Malli in her innermost self is 'imprisoned', and which she now embraces with courage and of her own volition.

The immutable power of fiction

"Tempests" is followed by "The Immortal Story", which was originally published in 1953.[21] Here we meet the enormously wealthy tea-trader Mr. Clay, who, like Soerensen, demands obedience and would like to control the world around him, but the "omnipotence" that Clay believes to be his is exercised by "ignoring that part of the world which lay outside the sphere of [his] power" (p. 157). Clay's power is based to an extreme degree on exclusion, and therefore he cannot – like Soerensen – realise a story.

Clay has just one passion: the million pounds he is worth, and which he calls "my brain and my heart" (p. 201). Because of this fixation, he lives a heartless life: "I have a distaste for the juices of the body. I do not like the sight of blood, I cannot drink milk, sweat is offensive to me, tears disgust me . . . in those relationships between people which they name fellowship, friendship or love, a man's bones themselves are . . . dissolved" (pp. 203–4). Clay is as dry as dust and hard as gold; like Martine and Philippa in "Babette's Feast" he is unacquainted with human love, and, like them, he lives a thoroughly ritualised life. Whereas Soerensen is able to create, Clay destroys; the house in which he lives previously belonged to a colleague whom he had ruined – suicide and the disintegration of a family being the consequence. Before Clay moved into the house, his colleague had smashed all the objects of art in it – underscoring the hostility to art in Clay's one-dimensional universe. It is also one-dimensionality that makes Martine and Philippa impervious to the art represented by Babette. Elishama, Clay's young clerk, feels that Clay's words are as if "spoken from the grave" (p. 175), and Clay's environment is indeed lifeless and deadly. Whereas Malli and Soerensen come together as pupil and master in a creative process, lifelessness binds Clay and Elishama together as employer and servant: "But since he himself did feel at home in the grave, he and his employer were at this moment brought closer together" (p. 175).

Like Clay, Elishama leads a secluded life and lives exclusively for his account books. Elishama is a Polish Jew whose family perished when he was a little boy – robbing him of every illusion about anything good in human relationships. There is no desire and no yearning in him and thus no possibility of a fulfilling reality; his status is comparable to Saufe's final stage in "The Diver". Elishama only wants to be left in peace and security, and this is one and the same as ruling out an earthly life. But by keeping the books of Clay's greed and thirst for power, Elishama is provided with the livelihood that makes it possible to live in peace and security. Elishama is called the Wandering Jew – he borrows the meaning from Ahasuerus – about which Karen Blixen elsewhere says: "The greatness of the figure is its isolation, its segregation from the universal human circumstances."[22] In the legend, Ahasuerus is condemned never to be able to die; in "The Immortal Story" Elishama seeks to shut death and suffering out of his life, but this is synonymous with a life that makes it difficult to die.

When he reaches the age of 70, Clay becomes ill and cannot sleep at night – the consequence of a thoroughly rationalised life that excludes dreaming. The same characteristic is shared by Lincoln's father in "The Dreamers" – a man who, as could also be said of Clay, represents northern Europe. Clay relieves his restless nights by instructing Elishama to read aloud from the company account books. But Clay's restricted world becomes evident when this factual 'literature' comes to an end and does not stand up to re-reading. Inadequate and transient are those world pictures – and the rendering thereof – which build exclusively on facts and the recordable. Sleepless, Clay wearies from hearing of the account books that have constituted his life; the spiritual poverty of that life thereby being open to scrutiny. Now dying, and having lived in a tomb, Clays asks Elishama if another kind of literature exists – a question that Elishama sees as an expression of "some deep need" (p. 159) and "emotions even, of which he had never spoken" (p. 201). This is reminiscent of the forgotten strings that, in "Babette's Feast", vibrate in Philippa's frustrated artistic nature, and also of Loewenhielm who, in the same tale, when approaching old age egoistically wants to partake of immortal life. Elishama has his past packed away in a red bag, in the form of an eternal tale written on a piece of paper which he had been given as a boy by an old Jewish man who had died on their flight from Poland. Using this he seeks to satisfy Clay's request, even though he is reluctant to do so:

> "*In order to help Mr. Clay, Elishama now took the bag from his box. Under other circumstances he would not have done so, for it brought with it notions of darkness and horror and the dim picture of a friend. Elishama did not want friends any more than Mr. Clay did. They were, to him, people who suffered and perished – the word itself meant separation and loss, tears and blood dripped from it.*" (p. 165)

The paper is a concentrated expression of the dark side of life, which Clay and Elishama shut out at great cost – the love and the shadows which have to be there to make for a rounded life: like the dark sheep thief in "The Ring" who represents death, incomprehensibility and love all in one, and thereby makes Lise's life complete. At the same time, the content of the piece of paper – Isaiah's prophecy – is an account of what happens once one has embraced the black aspect of life: "The wilderness and the solitary places shall be glad for them. And the desert shall rejoice, and blossom as the rose . . . Then shall the lame man leap as a hart . . . For in the wilderness shall waters break out. And streams in the desert" (pp. 165–6).[23] Confronted with the piece of paper and its text, which he does not tire of hearing, the dry Clay feels "painfully aware of his lameness" (p. 167).

Clay's strong emotional interest in Isaiah's prophecy alternates with a rejection of it on the intellectual level. He thinks it foolish to write about what is going to happen in the future and would rather hear about what has already happened; what has already befallen is another expression for lifelessness and for Clay's notion of stories as being a record of pure reality. He begins to tell Elishama the only story he has ever heard in his life, but it has never occurred to him that it is fiction. Nevertheless, he takes on the role of storyteller for the first time in his life, and that he is in the grip of imagination is underlined by the fact that his story is galvanised by the darkness: "Mr. Clay was so completely unaccustomed to telling a story, that it is doubtful whether he could have gone on with this one except in the dark" (p. 169).

Elishama informs Clay that his story has never *really* happened, but is a fairy tale told among sailors; it is only effective *because* it is a fairy tale. Seafaring folk do not concern themselves with realistic stories. Sailors will not talk about things that can happen in reality, because then it is not an authentic tale. Like the sailor on dry land who loses his *raison d'être*, a story will die without the element that the sea symbolises in Karen Blixen's writings: the dark, unpredictable and fairy-tale-like which provoke the reader's imagination.

The world of imagination is revealed to Clay; if he brings it in harmony with rationality, Isaiah's prophecy can be fulfilled. But Clay battens down the hatches and responds with a violent attempt at cementing his old world picture: he will make the sailors' story take place in reality and by so doing will destroy the fairy tale. Clay embarks upon "materializing a fantasy and changing a fable into fact" (p. 213), which conflicts with both reason and fantasy; Clay's display of power is thus doomed to failure. With his one-sidedness, Clay is powerless in the face of the world of art. As Elishama comments, the sailors' story will, on the contrary, be the end of Clay, because no one can take fiction and make it happen in reality, but fiction can repudiate the reality devoid of fantasy which Clay represents.

The sailors' story is about a wealthy old man who wants an heir, but is unable to have children with his young wife. In order to continue his family line, he hires the services of a sailor and pays him with fine food and expensive wine and a considerable amount of money. The sailor spends the night with "a lady" (p. 170), but it is not clear whether she is the young wife or a lady likewise hired by the wealthy old man. If she *is* the wife, the weakness in Clay's attempt to materialise the story is that *he* is not married, and therefore his choice of a whore for the female leading role infringes the story from the very outset. This uncertainty can also be seen as an insertion of ambiguity from Karen Blixen's hand, but it is a somewhat artificial attempt to resolve the inconsistency between the unmarried Clay and the husband in the sailors' story.

The story about an ageing gentleman who lets a younger man take his place in order to procreate is reminiscent of the lord of the manor's use of Adam in "Sorrow-Acre", but this old lord can rightfully realise his project because his power is Greek and aristocratic, whereas Clay's is purely bourgeois.

It is the irony of destiny that the female role is played by Virginie, the daughter of the very colleague ruined by Clay. Clay is unaware of her identity, whereas she plays along in order to take revenge on this man whom she considers to be her father's murderer. Clay personifies all that prevents a happy youth; but Virginie now experiences a happy youth anyway, in a certain respect, in that her meeting with the sailor is like a first tempestuous falling in love – in contrast to the whore's existence that became her lot after her father's death. Clay, who knows nothing about love, does not have the qualifications to anticipate this development in the scenario. Virginie sees it as her calling to be an actress and undertakes the assignment as a role by means of which theatre will catch up with the anti-art Clay via the back door. Moreover, Virginie comes from France, and she is confronted with Clay the Englishman in a contrast typical of Karen Blixen's stories: the 'French' represent the inclusion of all aspects of existence in a harmonious pattern, whereas the 'English' fragment their world. "Virginie had a taste for patterns; one of the things for which she despised the English was that to her mind they had no pattern in their lives" (p. 189). With his intention of destroying art by making it happen, Clay invites into his house the very substance of art, and Virginie's revenge is thus to subvert Clay's anti-art world. This act is inseparably bound up with the fact that at the same time Clay ushers in the very aspects of life that he has hitherto repressed. These are also manifest in the sailor with whom Virginie experiences love. He has recently spent a year alone on a deserted island, where he has become acquainted with silence – the optimum statement. He has a tattoo on the back of his hand: "a cross, a heart and an anchor" (p. 203); his character thus extends from the sky to the sea. Unlike Clay, the sailor is full of the sap of life, but as he is at the same time called a "boy" and it is said that he has just "come from a dungeon" (p. 199). He can also be seen as Clay's youth and passion, which never came to fruition. The sailor has "his big bones showing wherever his clothes did not cover him" (p. 199), and he is thus also that death which is part of a whole life and which now gives notice to Clay, who, with the sailor and Virginie under his roof, is heading towards his destruction. The destruction of Clay's dry world picture is the fulfilment of Isaiah's prophecy, and, via the sailor, the waters break out in Clay's desert – where Virginie is also in league with Isaiah, in that she retains "a flowerlike quality in her, as if there had been a large rose in water in the room" (p. 179).

The sailor is as spontaneous as a child, and at the same time he has a wild quality that also characterises Babette in "Babette's Feast" and the sheep thief in "The Ring". The sailor is "a huge wild animal" (p. 216); the eternal, pure natural force drives him – he is 'dehumanised' and therefore also described as "superhumanly big" (p. 222). The sailor is the material from which art is formed, and he therefore expresses himself like "a song, like a storm" (p. 221) – just as Malli in "Tempests". Like the most violent storm, an earthquake, he transforms everything for the whore Virginie, who now experiences sheer eroticism: "When in the course of the night the boy woke up, he behaved with the girl in his bed like a bear with a honeycomb, growling over her in a wild state of greed and ecstasy" (p. 219). Their anonymity here – the boy and the girl – emphasises that the earthquake is the Fall, which causes upheaval and renewal for all eternity. It takes place in the dark, as the sailor has given Clay his word that he will leave at dawn, and Virginie wants her face to be preserved in the sailor's memory as a blank page. It is also an assertion of love as the business of darkness and secrecy.

In the same way that old Jochum Hosewinckel livens up when he meets Malli, it is said of Clay when he meets the sailor that he "had strangely come to life" (p. 198). Contrary to his usual practice, he drinks wine while they eat a fine supper, and he enjoys "the unexpected strain of adventure in his sailor" (p. 205), knowing that he has found the right person for the story he wants to eradicate; but his enjoyment is also a consequence of the vitality that emerges as the fairy tale exerts its influence on him. Twofoldness recurs in relation to Virginie, who Clay, on the one hand, regards as a doll, but on the other hand we are told that "for the first time in his life he was impressed by a woman's beauty" (p. 213). Clay tells the sailor and Virginie that they are jumping-jacks in his all-controlling hand, but just afterwards his dressing-gown gets caught in the door, demonstrating that he is not master of the unexpected – it takes control of him. Spontaneity and imagination get the upper hand: "Now, as he was about to enter the heaven of his omnipotence, the Prophet laid his hand on his head and turned him into a child – in other words, the old stone-man was quietly entering his second childhood. He began to play with his story . . . " (p. 214). Babette's dinner has the same effect, as the parishioners in Berlevaag go into a second childhood. Whereas Clay had intended to stamp out the fiction, it now lives in him; he plays along. The story is more tenacious than Clay, and it is the story that undermines his world picture. When Elishama asks the sailor to tell the whole story of what he has experienced, in order to discharge Clay's mission, he refuses and maintains that there is a difference between fiction and reality. He adds that, moreover, no one would believe him if he told the story – meaning that sailors continue to believe in the fiction, thereby demonstrating its immortality. The sailor's response is also a repetition of the fact that sailors want to hear true stories, and recounting reality is not a true story.

Immortal forces overcome a power structure that is doomed to disaster for precisely the reason that it relies on the repression of the immortal. But we also see what he has repressed gaining a foothold in Clay's life, and therefore it is also a case of his liberation. That Isaiah's prophecy has been fulfilled is emphasised in several ways; towards the end of the tale Elishama repeats the words of the prophecy to himself and then hears the roar of great breakers in the sailor's shell – a sound that he calls a new voice in the house. And even Clay's garden appears to be watery and as if created anew: "Outside, the trees and flowers of Mr. Clay's garden were wet with dew, in the morning light they looked new and fresh, as if they had just this hour been created" (p. 229).

II Denial of Fate – "Babette's Feast"

Layers and episodes

When Karen Blixen decided, in 1949, that it was time to write for her American readers, an English friend, Geoffrey Gorer, voiced the opinion that she would not be able to write something acceptable to *The Saturday Evening Post*. Karen Blixen accepted the challenge and took note of Geoffrey Gorer's advice about what *was* acceptable: "Write about food . . . Americans are obsessed with food."[24] The outcome was "Babette's Feast", which *The Saturday Evening Post* turned down – as did *Good*

Housekeeping. In 1950 the tale was printed in *Ladies' Home Journal*,[25] which also published "The Ring" that year. *Ladies' Home Journal* had previously published "Sorrow-Acre" and later took other tales; together with "Babette's Feast", the magazine also accepted "Ghost Horses".[26]

"Babette's Feast" and "Ghost Horses" are among the finest examples of Karen Blixen's mastery of an uncomplicated narrative style – in contrast to the intricacy that many readers find in *Seven Gothic Tales*. "Babette's Feast" is not uncomplicated in the purely entertaining sense that Geoffrey Gorer imagined; it is a simple and straightforward narrative, which is nevertheless immensely capacious: a charming and credible story, but with a considerable underlying depth in which a sharp irony and dangerous forces are at work. On the surface "Babette's Feast" is the moving story of the Dean's daughters who are the very picture of self-sacrificing, charitable angels. Their faith offers them a commendable repudiation of love and art in favour of love of one's neighbour and hymn-singing. They open their home to the refugee Babette and give her shelter and work for life, and Babette offers up a fortune and repays their kindness by preparing a magnificent dinner to please the sisters and their congregation. But just a little scratch in the varnish, and a different story begins to surface; the story of a life spent in passivity and self-repression and of pent-up passions as the cost that brings the demons into play. It is a story about where the divine is actually to be found, and on this wider balance sheet the concept of sin is turned upside down out.

A consideration of the composition alone discloses the layers in the tale. It concentrates on three episodes in the sisters' lives. The first episode begins: "In the year of 1854, when Martine was eighteen and Philippa seventeen . . . " (p. 25), and we hear about their relationship with their admirers – the officer Lorens Loewenhielm and the opera singer Achille Papin, who come to Berlevaag within a year of each other. The second episode begins fifteen years after Papin's departure, more specifically "on a rainy June night of 1871" (p. 32) when Babette enters the sisters' house – sent by Papin. The sisters were by this time 35 and 34 years of age. Babette is introduced via Papin's letter to the sisters, and we are told about her acclimatisation to conditions in Berlevaag, the small Norwegian town where the tale takes place. Thereafter the tale jumps forwards to the final episode: "Babette remained in the house of the Dean's daughters for twelve years, until the time of this tale" (p. 35). This is the grand finale to the tale, the account of Babette's feast. We are now in 1883, the sisters are 47 and 46 years old. The tale ends where it begins – in a brief prelude the narrator has introduced the situation in the sisters' home twelve years after Babette's arrival, and here the narrator says: "Sixty-five years ago two elderly ladies lived in one of the yellow houses" (p. 23). In other words, the narrator is telling the story from the same time perspective that Karen Blixen had when writing it.

The story spans 29 years, but nothing is heard about what happens between the episodes – this being 15 years between the first and second episode and 12 years between the second and last episode. The events that are related are *the* events in the sisters' lives. What lies between – and, for that matter, before and after the 29 years – is uneventful. What happens in "Berlevaag life" (p. 55) (in the Danish version: "Berlevaag's inert little world") only happens with intrusion "from the great world outside Berlevaag" (p. 25): Loewenhielm from Sweden, and Papin from France. Babette arrives from France, as does the letter about the big lottery prize that enables her to plan the 'feast'. But the confrontation between the great world and the little world affords more than a minor comment on inertia.[27]

Heavenly love and blazing passion

When Loewenhielm sees Martine again at Babette's dinner, he asks himself what traces the intervening 30 years have left on her face – but "how serene was the forehead, how quietly trustful the eyes, how pure and sweet the mouth, as if no hasty word had ever passed its lips" (p. 55). Martine looks as pure and innocent as in her young days, and indeed she is, for nothing has changed since Loewenhielm was last there. Berlevaag lies just as it was, "a child's toy-town of little wooden pieces" (p. 23), and the congregation still look upon Martine and Philippa as children, "to them they were even now very small sisters" (p. 24). Neither has the sisters' home changed, the description reiterates its purity and 'pettiness':

> *"This low room with its bare floor and scanty furniture was dear to the Dean's disciples. Outside its windows lay the great world. Seen from in here the great world in its winter-whiteness was ever prettily bordered in pink, blue and red by the row of hyacinths on the window-sills. And in summer, when the windows were open, the great world had a softly moving frame of white muslin curtains to it."* (p. 49)

In the sisters' little world, which with the toy-town in mind is reminiscent of a doll's house, the greater perspective is kept out and down by purity and whiteness, but it is from the great world that Babette intrudes, and she is, as we shall see, conversely characterised by darkness and wildness. She comes to the toy-town of Berlevaag, from a Paris marked by bloody and dirty enormity, to be put in her place by the sisters. But in the finale to the tale she breaks out of this restriction, and in the sisters' eyes she seems to be "unusually large" (not in the English-language version, p. 72 in the Danish).

But Loewenhielm and Papin come to Berlevaag first. Loewenhielm falls in love with Martine, the feeling is reciprocated, but they remain completely passive and Loewenhielm goes away a frustrated man. Martine fails to meet destiny when love, in the form of Loewenhielm, shows itself, but the sisters' upbringing has not given them any means with which to act. Their father, the Dean, has kept them in an iron grip from which they never free themselves, and this renders Loewenhielm's and Papin's endeavours impossible:

> "To the Dean's congregation earthly love, and marriage with it, were trivial matters, in themselves nothing but illusions; still it is possible that more than one of the elderly Brothers had been prizing the maidens far above rubies and had suggested as much to their father. But the Dean had declared that to him in his calling his daughters were his right and left hand. Who could want to bereave him of them? And the fair girls had been brought up to an ideal of heavenly love; they were all filled with it and did not let themselves be touched by the flames of this world." (p. 25)

This is one of the most vehement descriptions of pernicious parental authority in Karen Blixen's entire literary output, and of destructive ecclesiastical authority. The description is of the same intensity as that in "Alkmene". To Karen Blixen, the possibility to oppose parents and other authoritative bodies is of absolutely vital significance for the independent development of a young person. In "The Ring" Lise's encounter with the earthly sheep thief enables her to free herself from the white doll-like world, which is compared to death; we have seen that the possibility is open at the end for Jensine in "The Pearls"; but Martine and Philippa remain their father's right and left hand, and even though there are times when it tugs intensely in them, their independence lies waste.

The total lack of sources in their background to facilitate independent development is also conveyed, with simple yet deep irony, in the description of the father himself. He talks in biblical quotations, a form of expression adopted by the entire congregation, who quote the Dean into the bargain. Moreover, Martine and Philippa are fixed from birth as a religious reference, in that they are named after Martin Luther and his friend Philip Melanchthon. Of Martine's and Philippa's exclusion from all that is part and parcel of being young we are told quite specifically that they "had never possessed any article of fashion" (p. 23), and "they were never to be seen at balls or parties" (p. 24). They are not to be found where earthly love is kindled, but it nevertheless forces its way into their lives in a potent form. For the one who is completely consumed by the heavenly light of love experiences the world's flames at close quarters, as revealed in the encounter between Philippa and Achille Papin.

Philippa sings divinely, and the opera singer Papin becomes her teacher – choosing to study the seduction duet from Mozart's opera *Don Giovanni* (1787); Philippa sings Zerlina, and "he himself, as often before, sang Don Giovanni's part" (p. 31). This proves to be a preposterous confrontation: "So the great French singer and the young Norwegian novice set to work together" (p. 30). Don Giovanni – the very embodiment of sensuality – face to face with purity and innocence personified. Philippa, who is kept in absolute ignorance of this aspect of life, reacts intensely during the duet, and when Papin is swept off his feet and kisses her, she abruptly cancels the singing lessons. Afterwards, Papin cannot remember having kissed Philippa – "I have no remembrance at all of the kiss!" (p. 32) – underscoring the subconscious, sensual powers which have been brought into play and which are at stake. Philippa, like Martine, is unable to do anything when love appears in her life, but she is affected by the episode. Martine feels "that the matter was deeper than it looked" (p. 32), and "she did not imagine that her sister might have been surprised and frightened by something in her own nature" (p. 32) – confirming that Philippa has indeed been profoundly shaken by this offer of earthly love. The Don Juan myth is also being used to tell about a dissonance *in* Philippa. Don Juan not only personifies the blazing passion that is possible in the life which Philippa sets aside, but he is also an illustration of the consequences of this rejection. In Søren Kierkegaard's *Enten/Eller* (*Either/Or*, 1843) it is stated in "Letters to A" about Don Juan (and Faust):

> "*When the idea of Don Juan emerged is not known; only this much is certain – that it is linked to Christianity and through Christianity to the Middle Ages ... The Middle Ages had to make the discord between the flesh and the spirit that Christianity brought into the world the subject of its reflection and to that end personified each of the conflicting forces. Don Juan, then, if I dare say so, is the incarnation of the flesh ... not until the*

contrast split even more deeply did Don Juan emerge as sensuality that is mortally opposed to spirit... When sensuousness manifests itself as that which must be excluded, as that with which the spirit does not wish to be involved... sensuousness takes this form, is the demonic... Faust and Don Juan are the Middle Ages' titans and giants, who in the grandness of their achievements are not different from those of antiquity, except admittedly in this, that they stand isolated, do not form an amalgamation of powers that only through amalgamation become heaven-storming... Don Juan, then, is the expression for the demonic qualified as the sensuous; Faust is the expression for the demonic qualified as the spiritual..." [28]

Mozart's *Don Giovanni* is also discussed in *Either/Or*, where the opera is the example par excellence, and is subjected to a detailed analysis. Throughout Karen Blixen's entire body of works, there is a confrontation with separation, including that which Søren Kierkegaard depicts in the above quotation. As we shall see, Babette is able to invalidate the separation, in that her dinner creates the conditions "in which one no longer distinguishes between bodily and spiritual appetite or satiety!" (p. 58). In a concrete sense, she becomes heaven-storming.

In *Begrebet Angest* (*The Concept of Anxiety*, 1844), Søren Kierkegaard elaborates on the concept of the demonic. The demonic can overtake a person if they disregard and repress their nature. It is where the natural, which for Søren Kierkegaard is also the sensual, is repressed to a high degree that it assumes unnatural, demonic forms, which can deprive the individual of power. The demonic is nature's revenge on the individual who has repressed it. When sensuality therefore makes its entrance in the Dean's home in the form of Don Juan, it shows to just what an extent it has been kept down. Don Juan is an image of the magnification and demonisation of sensuality which is the result of an upbringing and a faith that completely precludes earthly love, and here Karen Blixen's fiery portrait of passion also has the function of showing how dangerous this is. Philippa can meet the same fate as Don Juan; she, whose life is devoted to the heavenly light, may perish in the flames of hell.

In *The Concept of Anxiety*, Søren Kierkegaard discusses the negative concept of original sin, this being the human-created, but universally-applied erroneous interpretations of life that are superimposed on the natural original sin, by means of which the maturing individual experiences intensified difficulty in orienting his or her self. In the following quotation, "the ultimate more" is to be understood as the most intense form of negative hereditary sin: "Furthermore, the ultimate more in this respect is that an individual from his earliest awakening is placed and influenced in such a way that sensuousness for him has become identical with sinfulness, and this ultimate more will appear in the most painful form of collision if in the whole surrounding world he finds nothing that can give him support."[29] It is this same negative hereditary sin that is imposed on the sisters in "Babette's Feast". The demons with which they struggle are a consequence of this, and as they have no foundation for other interpretations and actions, they have to spend their entire lives shielding themselves behind whiteness and purity. Thus they cannot account for Papin: "Of this visitor from the great world the sisters spoke but little; they lacked the words with which to discuss him" (p. 32). For the same reason, Martine quickly shies away from the issue when Loewenhielm is mentioned.

In a contemporary novel, Martin A. Hansen's *Løgneren* (*The Liar*, 1950), the parish clerk and school teacher Johannes Vig reads Luke chapter 11, verses 14–27 in church – a text from the Scriptures to which he often returns in the novel. Johannes Vig has settled on the island of Sandø, but here, and in life in general, he feels like a migratory bird. He does not involve himself in any lasting way with anything, for he is afraid of sullying his mind. But the text is a reminder about the impossibility and danger of a 'pure' existence, and this becomes apparent to Johannes Vig in the following passage, which also incorporates the essence of the text from the Scriptures:

> "No! I decided not to say anything about the Sunday text. I was tempted, dangerously tempted, but what do you suppose I could really say about words like these: 'As the unclean spirit driven out of a man walketh through dry places, seeking rest, and findeth none, then says he, I will return to the house from whence I came.' What do you think of these words? Do you think that the parish clerk on Sandö can touch on so wild and strange an image? The unclean spirit, homeless and restless, driven out from his dwelling, a human being, wanders listlessly through waterless country, where there is nothing to drink, not even a dew drop, not even a blade of green grass. Have you ever thought of the evil spirit suffering, Nathanael?
>
> Then the unhappy, unclean spirit thinks again of the home he has left and turns back to find it, and when he finds it empty, swept, and garnished, 'then goeth he, and taketh with himself seven other spirits more wicked than himself, and they enter in and dwell there; and the last state of that man is worse than the first.'
>
> What ought I to have said about that, Nathanael? Of course, I could have lifted my chin, looked down my nose, and said: 'Take care, my friends! This is a warning to those who think they are clean: those who

have fought a strong and bitter fight, and feel themselves swept and garnished. Beware!"[30]

Nathanael is Johannes Vig's diary – and inner interlocutor. Acceptance of the "unclean" brings about that harmony in existence which Johannes Vig had not found before. He can now wholeheartedly involve himself in Sandø and thereby abandon himself to his earthly life. This does not happen for Martine and Philippa, but in Karen Blixen's work, in the same way, separation between the good and the evil always leads to the evil.

Love and art go hand-in-hand in "Babette's Feast". Philippa sets aside passion, but at the same time she abandons her natural talent for singing – the great artistic gift taken lovingly in hand by Papin in the lessons that she abruptly curtails. Before this happens, Papin has given Philippa a vivid description of her triumphal progress as a singer, which will culminate in Paris when she is led to the Café Anglais and thus to Babette:

> *"She would, he said, rise like a star above any diva of the past or present. The Emperor and Empress, the Princes, great ladies and bel esprits of Paris would listen to her, and shed tears. The common people too would worship her, and she would bring consolation and strength to the wronged and oppressed. When she left the Grand Opera upon her master's arm, the crowd would unharness her horses, and themselves draw her to the Café Anglais, where a magnificent supper awaited her."* (pp. 30–1)

What is missing in Berlevaag she will find in Paris: connoisseurs who can appreciate and celebrate her great art. This applies to the grand people, but the oppressed will also glean strength from her art, and it can be added that the manifestation of her art will liberate Philippa. With the image of Philippa being led to the Café Anglais where Babette is fulfilling her (culinary) art, Philippa and Babette are bound together, a connection which is elaborated later when, among other things, it becomes apparent that Babette's art was appreciated by the grandees at the same time as she was fighting to liberate the oppressed – a contradiction which Babette has no trouble in squaring.

Philippa is greatly affected by the proposition offered by Papin: "Philippa did not repeat these prospects to her father or her sister, and this was the first time in her life that she had had a secret from them" (p. 31). What Papin has to offer Philippa is so revolutionary that it will overturn the Dean's family world picture. Therefore it is not until many years later – after Babette's dinner in Berlevaag – that Philippa is able to feel that: "The stars have come nearer" (p. 63). As we have seen – and as the analysis of "The Ring" will develop – the 'secret' is of great value in Karen Blixen's universe. The concealment of Papin's proposition emphasises its great significance for Philippa; that it is the first time Philippa keeps something secret is also another testimony to how little her environment has fostered independence.

The taming of Babette

Philippa does not go to Babette in Paris, but Babette comes to Berlevaag. Philippa does not become the fêted artist who triumphs in the Café Anglais, but Babette becomes a fugitive who was *the* artist par excellence in France, but in Berlevaag is a housekeeper who toils for twelve years making ale-and-bread-soup and in all probability continues to do so after her sumptuous dinner. In a sense, Babette's arrival in Berlevaag is a consequence of Philippa's refusal to fulfil herself in Paris. It is, to say the least, a mismatched alliance: the life-renouncing sisters and Babette who could create the ultimate gratification.

It is (of course) Papin who sends Babette to the sisters in Norway. This happens despite Philippa's rebuff fifteen years earlier, but he does *not* imagine that circumstances in Berlevaag have remained unchanged; on the contrary, to him Philippa is an image of love and fruitfulness: "When tonight I think of you, no doubt surrounded by a gay and loving family ... " (p. 34), as he writes in the letter which Babette brings with her. In the letter he expresses the hope that the sisters will "save the life of a Frenchwoman" (p. 33), ignorant of the lifelessness in Berlevaag, which is also an expression of the isolation that is the fate of the exile. As a Communard, and thus participant on the rebellious Paris Commune's side in the civil war of 1871, Babette has had to flee France after their defeat. Both her husband and son, who were also Communards, have been shot, and it is emphasised that Babette has lost everything. She has – as when she later uses her entire fortune on her dinner – staked everything for the sake of freedom. The civil war was – if it is possible to quantify such events – monstrously brutal, and Babette has, without thought for her own safety, in aristocratic fashion been in the thick of it: "I stood upon a barricade; I loaded the gun for my menfolk!" (p. 67; the Danish version, p. 73, adds: "my arms were black, as now, with gunpowder. I stepped in blood, my stockinged feet were soaked in it.").

Babette says this to Philippa and Martine in the kitchen just after the dinner, hence the little, but significant, "as now", linking the rebellion in Paris to the rebellious dinner. From the bloody and black reality in Paris during the civil war to the purity and whiteness of Berlevaag there is a world of difference. It is the home in Berlevaag, fiercely warding off "the flames of this world" (p. 25), to which Babette comes, the Babette of whom Papin also writes: "She herself was arrested as a Pétroleuse – (which word is used here for women who set fire to houses with petroleum) . . . " (p. 33).

There are 'good' reasons for Babette's presence in the sisters' house, but they are not the essential point. Like a Trojan horse, this fiery soul has been let in and, fundamentally, she has been there all along; in the prelude to the story, which describes the circumstances in the house twelve years after Babette's arrival, we are told that:

> "These two ladies had a French maid-of-all work, Babette.
>
> It was a strange thing for a couple of Puritan women in a small Norwegian town; it might even seem to call for an explanation. The people of Berlevaag found the explanation in the sisters' piety and kindness of heart. For the old Dean's daughters spent their time and their small income in works of charity; no sorrowful or distressed creature knocked on their door in vain. And Babette had come to that door twelve years ago as a friendless fugitive, almost mad with grief and fear.
>
> But the true reason for Babette's presence in the two sisters' house was to be found further back in time and deeper down in the domain of human hearts." (p. 24)

The allusion at the end of this passage is to where it all started, namely the love and art personified by Loewenhielm and Papin. Babette's adversity and the sisters' kindness to her is the surface explanation, where here both parties' care for the needy unites them, but fundamentally Babette is present as the other side of the sisters – as that love and art which via rejection of Loewenhielm and Papin was consigned to the darkness of their hearts, a place from which it is not until twelve years after Babette's arrival that love and art appear again in the form of the insurgent dinner.

The way in which Babette is treated is, in a sense, merely a repetition of the treatment of Loewenhielm and Papin; they are sent away, she is put firmly in her place *within* the household. The sisters consistently carry into effect their determined resolve to educate Babette in their faith: "They silently agreed that the example of a good Lutheran life would be the best means of converting their servant. In this way

Babette's presence in the house became, so to say, a moral spur to its inhabitants" (p. 36). The concrete expression for this is their instruction to Babette that their food must be "as plain as possible" (p. 36); they explain to her that food has no significance for them and that "luxurious fare was sinful" (p. 36). It is not so strange that Babette's face thereupon becomes "absolutely expressionless" (p. 36), as in this the sisters are depriving her of everything through which she has expressed herself at the Café Anglais. Babette has, however, one qualification for complying with the sisters' request for ale-and-bread-soup, in that when she was young she "had been cook to an old priest who was a saint" (p. 36). But this merely heightens her contrast to the sisters: in the priest, Babette has had an authority equal to that which the sisters have in their father, the Dean, but, unlike the sisters, Babette has broken away by taking the leap and going to the Café Anglais (the leap which Philippa did not take).

Babette the world-class artist – "the greatest culinary genius of the age" (p. 58) – suffers the fate of making ale-and-bread-soup for 12 years, whereas previously she daily conjured miracles in her kitchen. Imagine if Maria Callas had been set to sing nothing but litanies for 12 years. There is no scope whatsoever in Berlevaag for Babette's self-expression, and her presence is an illustration of the repression of love and art that is found in the lives of the pious sisters. Babette is obliged – like Martine and Philippa – to put aside her natural predisposition and talents. She is actually blatantly exploited, which becomes apparent when she wins the lottery and the sisters' egoistic concern is about how her probable departure will affect *them*:

> "*The ten thousand francs which made her rich – how poor did they not make the house she had served! One by one old forgotten cares and worries began to peep out at them from the four corners of the kitchen. The congratulations died on their lips, and the two pious women were ashamed of their own silence ...* (the Danish text pp. 48–9 adds: *they would again have to soak their own split cod and cook their own ale-and-bread-soup.) Indeed, indeed, lotteries were ungodly affairs.*" (p. 41)

What the sisters had been – "precious for their dear father's sake" (p. 24) and their father's right and left hand – Babette has become for them; the pattern is repeated.

Of Babette's assimilation the narrator is able to draw the conclusion: "Babette had arrived haggard and wild-eyed like a hunted animal, but in her new, friendly surroundings she soon acquired all the appearance of a respectable and trusted servant" (p. 35). In this simplicity there is deep irony: the wildness – which again characterises Babette when she accomplishes her dinner – is tamed, and Babette is reduced to an implement. Like a hunted wild animal she is described in the same terms as the sheep thief in "The Ring", who likewise represents all that is 'dangerous' for a white and thereby deathly-still environment. And the colour black characterises the sheep thief and Babette alike. Her yearning for the opportunity of self-expression can be provoked by the mention of Paris – so "the word Paris called Babette out of her isolation" (not in the English-language version, p. 70 in the Danish version) – but the sisters would also find her "lost in the study of a heavy black book" (p. 38), which is undoubtedly a book about finer culinary practise, but it could just as well be the *Koran*.

Kaaba and the cornerstone

The members of the congregation are delighted that the transfer of domestic work to Babette has released the sisters from the role of "Martha", enabling them to be "two fair Marys" who have time to talk with the brotherhood about "heavenly matters" (p. 37). The congregation thinks constantly in biblical terms, and here the reference is to the story about Jesus' visit to the sisters Mary and Martha: while Mary takes time to talk with Jesus, Martha carries on with the domestic work, and when Martha complains to Jesus that her sister is letting her do all the work alone, Jesus simply replies that "one thing is needful: and Mary hath chosen that good part, which shall not be taken away from her."[31]

The Bible story makes us see Babette as a 'sister' to Martine and Philippa, but she represents the aspect *in* the sisters that they dismiss in order to engross themselves completely in the heavenly. Babette is entrusted with the work belonging to life on earth, again underlining the separation between the earthly and the heavenly – of which nothing good comes. Babette proves indispensable because she provides the congregation and the sisters with their daily ale-and-bread-soup, enabling them to devote themselves entirely to the heavenly; this is recognised by the brotherhood in their assessment of Babette in another biblical light: "The stone which the builders had almost refused had become the headstone of the corner" (p. 37). With this more or less verbatim Bible passage, Babette is seen as the stone that, in various forms of expression, is referred to a number of times in both *The Old Testament* and *The New Testament*, where the stone is partly God, partly Jesus. The Bible states that for those who are believers, the stone is elevating, as it is a case of being "built upon the foundation of the apostles and prophets, Jesus Christ himself being the chief corner stone; / In whom all the building fitly framed together groweth unto an holy temple in the Lord: / In whom ye also are builded together for an habitation of God through the Spirit."[32] For the disbeliever, however, the stone will be "a stone of stumbling, and a rock of offence . . . "[33]

For the congregation in "Babette's Feast" there is security in seeing Babette as the foundation in the sisters' holy temple and themselves as pillars therein, but Martine and Philippa, who know Babette better, are not so sure; they are afraid that the stone could bring about the downfall of their house, because *they* see in Babette a stone of another and dangerous cast: "The ladies of the yellow house were the only ones to know that their cornerstone had a mysterious and alarming feature to it, as if it was somehow related to the Black Stone of Mecca, the Kaaba itself" (p. 37). Like Muhammad, Babette has been driven out of *her* Mecca and can therefore read the *Koran* with longing. Even though Karen Blixen could be critical of Islam, there was also something about it that attracted her and it is most likely these qualities that Babette longs for.

In *Letters from Africa, 1914–1931*, Karen Blixen writes of followers of Islam: "Their morals are very charitable because unlike Christians they have no concept of *sin*,"[34] and in the essay "Farah" she goes into more detail:

> "*I have been told that the word 'Islam' in itself means submission: the Creed may be defined as the religion which ordains acceptance. And the Prophet does not accept with reluctance or with regret but with rapture. There is in his preaching, as I know it from his unlearned disciples, a tremendous erotic element . . . In contrast to many modern Christian ideologies, Islam does not occupy itself with justifying the ways of God to man; its Yes is universal and unconditional. For the lover does not measure the worth of his mistress by a moral or social rod. But the mistress, by absorbing into her own being the dark and dangerous phenomena of life, mysteriously transluminates and sanctifies them, and imbues them with sweetness . . . I imagined that just as the erotic aloofness of the founder of Christianity has left his disciples in a kind of void, or of chronic uneasiness and remorse, within this province of life, so has the formidable, indomitable potency of the Prophet pervaded his followers and made mighty latent forces in them fetch headway.*"[35]

By linking Babette and the Prophet Muhammad, a contrast is provided to Martine's and Philippa's religion and the thereby associated mode of existence – the contrast highlighting abandonment to and fulfilment of every aspect of life on earth. This insistence on acceptance of life *all told* is a recurrent theme in Karen Blixen's writings, and in a letter from Africa she has expressed it very simply: "I believe that life demands of us that we love it, not merely certain sides of it and not only one's own ideas and ideals, but life itself in all its forms, before it will give us anything in return, and when you mention my philosophy of life, I have no other than that . . . "[36]

The diabolical claim

The colour black is in evidence again when Philippa and Martine see Babette sitting "on the three-legged kitchen chair, her strong hands in her lap and her dark eyes wide open, as enigmatical and fatal as a Pythia upon her tripod" (p. 38). Yet again Babette is magnified via the power of mythology, she is supported by the soothsayer Pythia and thereby Pythia's commander, Apollo, god of the fine arts and the leader of the Muses. Now the moment of truth is heralded when Babette will give free reign to the entire register of her art in her dinner. The reference to Apollo is chosen because he was also, at the same time, god of order and peace and illness and death; in other words, he united life in all its forms, in contrast to the Christian dualism characteristic of the Dean's home in Berlevaag.

The sight of the drooping Babette alarms the sisters, and they have to acknowledge that there are aspects to her of which they have no knowledge or cannot control: "At such moments they realized that Babette was deep, and that in the soundings of her being there were passions, there were memories and longings of which they knew nothing at all. A little shiver ran through them, and in their hearts they thought: 'Perhaps after all she had indeed been a Pétroleuse'" (p. 38). This is where the fiery soul is awakened in Babette, and *that* is the devil's affair.

That "lotteries were ungodly affairs" (p. 41) is the sisters' explaining-away of the unexpected prize that creates chaos in their exceedingly well-regulated world. But the ungodly/diabolical is also the form in which the recurrent suppression shows itself, and last, but not least, the diabolical is in a positive sense the unexpected, surprising and unpre-dictable which ensures that life does not stagnate in well-regulated and routine rationalisation. In Karen Blixen's universe the diabolical is prin-

cipally a creative, constructive factor, and therefore it makes sense that
the artist Babette should be in collusion with the devil and with his help
creates her divine meal.

To the sisters, and in actual fact, the dinner is "a thing of incalculable
nature and range" (p. 45) and therefore initiated by "dangerous powers"
(not in the English-language version, p. 53 in the Danish version). The
sisters want to celebrate their father's centenary by inviting the congregation to a plain supper, but Babette asks to be allowed to cook "a real
French dinner" (p. 42) – this is the second time Philippa hears about
French cuisine, the first being when Papin holds out the prospect of a
"magnificent supper" awaiting her at Café Anglais. That it should be
genuinely French is not chosen by chance, as Paris and France had a
special significance for Karen Blixen, she wrote in a letter from Africa
to her sister Ellen Dahl:

> "Even when I was there in war time in 1915 I felt that Paris was illumi-
> nated with a splendour possessed by no other places, and the solemnity of
> the war seemed not at all in contrast to the beauty and life of Paris, and
> that indeed I think is the greatest charm of Paris and of France as a whole
> – and the great gift of the south, where everything is in harmony; they can
> assimilate all the various elements of life into one beauty. Everything that
> in less perfect natures exists in a state of contradiction: body and spirit,
> nature and ideal, theory and practice, art and life, life and death, – there
> becomes the most delightful harmony … To me France always represents
> the Holy Land; from there arise beauty and liberty, the most divine forces
> of life … "[37]

The daughters' celebration of their father's centenary testifies to his con-
tinuing hold over them, but for Babette it is an opportunity to accomplish
the real French synthesis – against his regime. The sisters, however, do
not immediately give permission for the dinner; first Babette has to penetrate their defences. She breaks through with means from the great
world outside (pp. 42–4): the colour black – "Babette's dark eyes were as
eager and pleading as a dog's"; the diabolical unpredictability – "the very
strangeness of the request disarmed them" ; and of course "with classical French eloquence". This persuasion, the first step in the revolt against
the Dean's regime, is conducted with the same vigour as when Babette
fought against a comparable oppression: "Had she stepped forth like this,
in 1871, to plant a red flag on a barricade?". Babette's isolation in
Berlevaag is underlined by the fact that the letter from France inform-
ing her about the lottery prize is her first contact with the outside world
for twelve years. Armed with the letter, she is now for the first time able

to make a prayer: "Ladies! Had she ever, during twelve years, asked you a favor? No! And why not? Ladies, you who say your prayers every day, can you imagine what it means to a human heart to have no prayer to make? What would Babette have had to pray for? Nothing! Tonight she had a prayer to make, from the bottom of her heart". This says everything about how disarmed Babette has been, but at the same time that what had been consigned to the darkness of her heart – love and art – now irrefutably claims advance to the forefront. The oppression has been flagrant, but therefore there is so much power behind Babette's request that the sisters have to yield: "Their consent in the end completely changed Babette. They saw that as a young woman she had been beautiful. And they wondered whether in this hour they themselves had not, for the very first time, become to her the 'good people' of Achille Papin's letter" (pp. 43–4). Their consent releases those powers that Babette gave free rein in her youth, but it is also apparent that the sisters have deprived her of these powers; it is not until now that they make allowance for everything that Babette represents.

As soon as preparations for the dinner are underway, Babette's transformation continues. By the time the goods – from Paris – have arrived, Babette has swelled, which shows how 'shrivelled' she had been: "By this time Babette, like the bottled demon of the fairy tale, had swelled and grown to such dimensions that her mistresses felt small before her" (p. 45). Babette becomes empowered and is magnified beyond her individuality as in a fairy tale; in Karen Blixen's universe the fairy-tale aspect, as often is the case with the mythological, is a magnifying, enriching and primary expression. It is repeatedly stressed that Babette 'grows' in tact with the realisation of the dinner, and when it has been accomplished she is able to declare triumphantly: "I am a great artist!" (p. 66). In contrast to this assertion, on several occasions Babette calls the sisters "my little ladies" (e.g., p. 68).

The serpent in Berlevaag

Merely the sight of the goods that Babette brings into the house strikes at the very core of the sisters. Martine is paralysed by the arrival of the wine, and in the later darkness of evening she is deprived the power of speech:

> "*Late in the evening she opened the door to a ring, and was once more faced with the wheelbarrow, this time with a red-haired sailor-boy behind*

it ... The youth grinned at her as he lifted a big, undefinable object from the barrow. In the light of the lamp it looked like some greenish-black stone, but when set down on the kitchen floor it suddenly shot out a snake-like head and moved it slightly from side to side. Martine had seen pictures of tortoises, and had even as a child owned a pet tortoise, but this thing was monstrous in size and terrible to behold. She backed out of the kitchen without a word. " (pp. 45–6)

Martine has neither the words nor the courage to tell her sister what she has seen, but the tortoise is nevertheless a demonic magnification of the one she owned as a child. The dark colouring of the "stone" claims kinship to the black stone in Mecca, and there is also a snake moving within it. Martine knows about the snake's seductive and fatal demonology from the Bible, although she has also read that the Lord protects those who put their trust in Him: "There shall no evil befall thee, neither shall any plague come nigh thy dwelling. / For he shall give his angels charge over thee, to keep thee in all thy ways. / They shall bear thee up in their hands, lest thou dash thy foot against a stone. / Thou shalt tread upon the lion and adder; the young lion and the dragon shalt thou trample under feet."[38]

But that evil which Martine, trusting to the Lord, has trodden under-foot has now become a plague in her own house; she lies awake, not falling asleep until the morning hours and then only to have a night-mare "in which she saw Babette poisoning the old Brothers and Sisters, Philippa and herself" (p. 46).

Martine does not imagine that the snake's poison is also an antidote, but there are other than Christian notions about the snake behind Babette's (and Karen Blixen's) use of it: "That the snake in European folk tradition is designated as evil, is in all probability the result of Christian influence ... Cutting across this tradition is a broad stream of traditions about the snake as an agent by means of which to acquire wealth, wisdom and health or recovery from illness."[39]

In *Out of Africa*, Count Schimmelmann is under Christian influence, in that he turns vehemently against the snake in order to maintain a sound conscience and the distinction between good and evil, but a showman, the proprietor of an itinerant menagerie, tells him that "indeed it is the best advice that I can give you: You should love the snakes ... nearly every time that we ask the Lord for a fish, he will give us a serpent."[40] The proprietor of the menagerie's love of the snake and the Count's poisonous appraisal of it recurs in Sophus Claussen's poem

"Mennesket" (Man) from the volume *Diableries* (1904), a veritable homage to the snake's (and dragon's) blazing and divine passion:

"I love the dragon's wildness, and the serpent sting only strikes
those who look at snakes with venomous eyes.

And I hold golden celebrations with the god or beast,
who is the silent pulse in the monster of the world.

I even love the flame and venom, which the snake hisses,
and I blow it away. Do you want to know what I blow?

Yes, when it snorted venomous and murderous in its slough,
I whispered like the priest: *'It is*
*   Love, all of it.'*

And when I glimpsed the sparkle of the lovely mermaid tail,
I heard the sighing of forests and the song of nightingales.

Once, from pure love, we will each other's mind capture.
Then I will whisper to it: 'Divine snake!'

'Divine snake! I was robbed of my strength,
when I did not see the living, which
*   gleamed deep in the foliage.'*

Then it will become a divinity. Not the dragon, wicked and barbed!
The instrument I blow is called the wonder-horn." [41]

That Sophus Claussen had been of significance to Karen Blixen's notion of snakes and demonology is clearly evident from letters written to her mother, Ingeborg Dinesen: "I so much regret that I did not manage to ask you to send me Sophus Claussen's *Diableries* . . . I find it hard to live without it. 'Aphrodite's Vapors' and 'Man' are a kind of gospel for me."[42] And she writes about the "many times I have thought about and been comforted by the poem about the divine serpent . . . "[43] In a letter to her brother, Thomas Dinesen, she writes that it is costly to talk with the Devil, and in that connection she quotes the following from Sophus Claussen's poem "Diableries": "the Devil is expensive to talk to, a sparkling glimpse of his fiery tail of stars costs more than most people can pay."[44] Karen Blixen's point is that this productive contact with the Devil demands a specific investment of personal strength, which at that moment in time she did not consider herself to have at her disposal, but with which she subsequently equips Babette. As is apparent from the passage quoted from the poem "Man", heaven and hell are also inviolably linked for Sophus Claussen, subtly emphasised in the final two lines of the poem "Diableries": "I can tell from your divine smile,/that the devil's mischief has your ear."[45] Which is how one can imagine Babette as she prepares her dinner, but it is also true of those who eat it!

Armament and witches' Sabbath

The sisters' reaction to Babette's approaching dinner is a resolute arma-ment. Shortly before they take their places at the table, they join the congregation in singing "one of the Master's own hymns", the third verse of which asks: "Wouldst thou give a stone, a reptile / to thy pleading child for food?" (p. 50),[46] and we are told that this verse "went straight to Martine's heart" (p. 50). After the serpent had seduced Eve, God's punishment was to turn it into a reptile, and the serpent is to be found in one of the stones which Babette brings into the house. Martine can momentarily derive support from this spiritual song, but the inex-orable logic in "Babette's Feast" is that because Martine lives solely from (ale-and-) bread (-soup) and spiritual nourishment, stone and reptile is exactly what she *gets*.

During the course of her preparations, Babette gradually takes posses-sion of the house; the sisters sense the sinister atmosphere thickening, and they protect themselves by doing "their best to embellish the domain left to them" (p. 49). They make use of an old Christian expe-dient by hanging "a garland of juniper round their father's portrait on the wall" (p. 49), so that the Brothers and Sisters can feel at ease by looking at "the face of their beloved Master, wreathed with evergreen" (p. 49). As a means to counteract the dark powers, the Dean is elevated in a divine light – he is treated on a par with the Virgin Mary, whose divinity is celebrated by decorating her image with sprays of juniper.[47] But the Dean has been instrumental in his own elevation – stories are told during the dinner about his "miracles", one such taking place when he had promised to give a sermon in a church on the other side of the fjord, even if he had to "come to them walking upon the waves" (p. 57). It is therefore not surprising that grace before the meal is spoken in the Dean's own words. As well as encircling the Dean's portrait with a garland of juniper, the sisters burn juniper twigs as if at Mass, but also "to make the room smell nice" (p. 49). They are also following a more widespread popular tradition in which the burning of juniper twigs has been "much used in wintertime as incense to counteract unpleasant smells indoors, and after spring cleaning . . . the smoke drove out flies, mosquitoes, spiders and other insects from bedrooms and furniture."[48]

Juniper has been used as a natural remedy against contagious illnesses and poisonous bites, and to "extinguish the evil lust".[49] For the superstitious, juniper has been attributed the power to ward off sorcery, including protection from witchcraft.

The sisters' reaction has to be considered in light of the fact that they actually imagined the worst – that they were in the process of turning their father's house over "to a witches' sabbath" (p. 46). In their eyes, Babette and the red-haired ship's boy who had brought the turtle into the house and who assists Babette before and during the dinner are transformed into "some witch with her familiar spirit" (p. 48). They find themselves in a difficult situation because they can undoubtedly clearly remember God's commandment: "Thou shalt not suffer a witch to live."[50]

Karen Blixen's conception of the witch, and therefore her idea in turning Babette into a witch, is nevertheless the very opposite of the Bible's. In the essay "Daguerreotypes", which was published in 1951, the year after "Babette's Feast", she stressed the mutinous and liberating aspect of the witch: "But there was a woman who, long before the words 'emancipation of women' came into use, existed independently of a man and had her own center of gravity. She was the witch."[51] The witch is a seductress and directs her desire towards the one who is in a position to satisfy it, this being the devil. Here Karen Blixen sees the following consolation for the male: "the basis, indeed the prerequisite for the witch's entire activity is the circumstance that the devil is masculine."[52] Like Babette, the witch is characterised by the colour black, in that Karen Blixen proclaims the witch to be "a black guardian angel" and indeed even "a bat on a dark night"[53] – evoking the vampire which, like Babette, reigns in the darkness because it is inhibited by the light, the white. Finally, Karen Blixen emphasises a characteristic of the witch with which she has equipped Babette in full measure: "She is a housewife to the hilt: fire and fireplace are precious to her and the cauldron is indispensable."[54]

In "Daguerreotypes" Karen Blixen refers to a specific historical event where a woman was convicted of being a witch: "The judges at the witch trials who used every means to procure the witch's confession that on the island of Samsø she had worked magic which kept Princess Anne from her journey to her bridegroom, James VI of Scotland, refrained from acquiring the magic recipe itself from her."[55] The judges are just as alarmed by the witch's recipe as Martine and Philippa are by Babette's preparation for her dinner, and in a way they are confronted with the same woman. The witch trials to which Karen Blixen refers were some of the most comprehensive in Danish history and attributed 'responsibility' for the many misfortunes that befell a fleet which, in 1589, was to sail Princess Anne across to her husband-to-be, James VI, the son of Mary Stuart. The fleet was hit by a storm, and following a number accidents on the ships many sailors were killed, all of which resulted in the Princess being obliged to spend the winter in Oslo. This was a great ignominy for Admiral Peder Munk, until the facts of the matter were disclosed: "Karen Vævers had sent her 'boy', a little demon familiar . . . out to the ships in an empty beer barrel, and Maren Bryggers had made the storm in some pots with water, where she had played with eggshells representing ships."[56] Karen Vævers and Maren Bryggers were among the 13 women who were burnt as witches; it is clear from "Daguerreotypes" that Karen Blixen knew about the case. And with the repeated emphasis in "Babette's Feast" that the ship's boy is Babette's "familiar spirit" (p. 48) or "red-haired familiar" (p. 54), it can be surmised that Karen Vævers and the boy she placed on the ships as her demon familiar had been in Karen Blixen's mind when she paired Babette and the red-haired ship's boy.

According to Thomas Aquinas' witch theory in *Summa Theologica*[57] the witch is the spawn of the devil: the devil changes into a demon and then to a woman who, at night, wrests the seed from the male when she, an incubus, descends upon him in his sleep; subsequently, the devil changes into a man who transmits the seed to a woman – and the issue is a witch, wherewith, according to Thomas Aquinas, evil comes into the world. But originally the idea of the witch was an element in a fertility cult that was inflexibly hostile to and defiant of Christianity and the well-ordered religious social structure. The evil is the monk's construction: he desires the woman in dream/nightmare and abhors her when in the waking state, but the witch herself is satisfied with carnal lust, and she thereby subscribes to an ancient tradition: "The fertility goddess from Crete is equipped with the classic attributes of the witch: serpents and sexuality."[58]

The witch implements black magic and carries out her fertility rituals especially in the Black Mass, which is called the witches' sabbath. The prerequisite for participation in the witches' sabbath was to make a pact with the devil: in return for promising him your soul, you were ensured eternal prosperity. The devil could make you wealthy; therefore it is hardly surprising that Martine and Philippa consider Babette's lottery winnings to be "ungodly". The pact was effected by the new witch, with her own blood, entering her name in "the devil's big book",[59] which could also have been in mind when Babette was set to read the heavy black book. Once the pact had been entered into, "admission was given to a circle of witches (13 in all, 12 witches and a leader. This is called a witches' coven) . . . Admission to a witches' coven sanctioned participation in the witches' sabbath."[60] The witches' coven was an ironic replica of Jesus and his 12 disciples, and the witches' sabbath proceeded in total contradiction to the Jewish Sabbath Feast and the Christian Eucharist. It took place at night in the moonlight, the menu might include children, toads, serpents and bat stew, to which black wine was drunk, and the night culminated in a manifestation of free sexuality in which the devil was the central figure.

The sisters' notion that they are faced with a witches' sabbath also comes to expression in their speculation as to what they will be given to eat. They see the snake in the turtle, and just before the dinner "frogs and snails" (p. 47) come to mind, while after the dinner they compare Babette to an African chief who serves up, at a feast, his infant grandchild. They come to an agreement with the Brothers and Sisters to remain completely silent on the subject of what they are given to eat. Moreover, "we will cleanse our tongues of all taste and purify them of all delight or disgust of the senses" (p. 47), and "they would not even give it a thought!" (p. 55) – they endeavour to counter the witchcraft by means of silence and the greatest possible displacement. The congregation also has the pious wish to experience a repetition of "the wedding of Cana" (p. 55) at which Jesus manifested his glory by turning water into wine – yet another defence mechanism – but here, however, revelation through wine is not alien to Babette, it is merely her objective that is different. Karen Blixen perhaps also wanted to lead the reader's thoughts to the account in *The Gospel According to St Luke* about Jesus attending a feast on the Sabbath, and there – through a parable involving a feast – teaches the assembly about humility: "For whosoever exalteth himself shall be abased; and he that humbleth himself shall be exalted."[61] On this same occasion, Jesus draws up the rigorous requirement of selfless devotion he expects of anyone who wants to be his disciple: "If any man come to me, and hate not his father, and mother, and wife, and children, and brethren, and sisters, yea, and his own life also, he cannot be my disciple . . . So likewise, whosoever he be of you that forsaketh not all that he hath, he cannot be my disciple."[62] In contrast to this, Babette's dinner is unmitigated self-fulfilment and flies in the face of self-abasement and self-denial, by means of which she eliminates that hatred which many of the Brothers and Sisters have built up towards one another. There is, however, one detail in *The Gospel According to St Luke* to which Babette would be able to subscribe: Jesus instructing the Pharisees that healing on the Sabbath is allowed! As Babette is serving a table with twelve settings, the Last Supper is also brought to mind, where Jesus says: "For whether is greater, he that sitteth at meat, or he that serveth? is not he that sitteth at meat? but I am among you as he that serveth."[63] Prior to the Crucifixion and eternal life, Jesus makes his body and his blood accessible to posterity through bread and wine; the Eucharist in the Lutheran tradition is seen as a proclamation of the remission of sins. Babette's 'Eucharist' does indeed give the Brothers and Sisters absolution, but here the sin is of a different calibre, being an offence against the earthly life of which Babette's food and wine is an incarnation.

Even though these underlying biblical images are elements that highlight Babette's purpose, they are, however, principally part of the religious and otherworldly philosophy that the tale treats ironically. Eternal life and self-denial are not Babette's calling; she *wants* the heavenly, but here on earth. And if a notion of the witches' sabbath is an expression of Martine's and Philippa's frustrations, it is simultaneously and more profoundly an image of what Babette actually carries into effect in order to achieve her objective. Karen Blixen's use of witch mythology also takes the witches' coven into account: twelve at the table with Babette as the thirteenth, overseeing the progress of the dinner, blow by blow, from the kitchen. From her domain she introduces sensuality and worldly delights behind the backs of the guests, and in so doing she breaks the promise they have made to one another that during the dinner they will keep to "the higher things of praise and thanksgiving" (p. 47) as dictated to them by the Dean. When Babette worked at Café Anglais, it was said of her that she could turn a dinner into "a love affair of the noble and romantic category in which one no longer distinguishes between bodily and spiritual appetite or satiety!" (p. 58), and she repeats this unity on the Dean's centenary anniversary when the guests are brought together "bodily as well as spiritually hand in hand" (p. 63). Despite their advanced years, they allow themselves to be bewitched: "Skipper Halvorsen and Madam Oppegaarden suddenly found themselves close together in a corner and gave one another that long, long kiss, for which the secret uncertain love affair of their youth had never left them time" (pp. 61–2), the consequence of which is that "time itself had merged into eternity" (p. 61), but in the sense expressed by the

Danish poet Emil Aarestrup: "And there the long witch's kiss will create / eternity for me on earth."[64]

The moment of absolution

During Babette's dinner, body and soul, earth and heaven, art and life, time and eternity melt together and generate the freedom, happiness and feeling of affinity that wells up in the Brothers and Sisters, whose daily situation is one of segregation and fragmentation. They are for a while liberated from "the vain illusions of this earth"(p. 62), in that Babette's revelation of the heavenly here on earth leads them to see "the universe as it really is. They had been given one hour of the millennium" (p. 62). Babette's revelation makes them feel that "the stars have come nearer" (p. 63), and it is no surprise that the dinner triggers off a snow storm – earth and heaven merge into one.

The food and drink that Babette serves is – naturally – the best. The turtle becomes a superb soup, and one of the other courses is, moreover, "Cailles en Sarcophage" (p. 58). Quail in sarcophagus – it is not inconceivable that Babette attempts to let the destiny-shunning see themselves reflected in this bizarre image of lifelessness. Furthermore, 'sarcophagus' has an original meaning which exposes the Brothers and Sisters' denial of the flesh: the term actually referred to coffins made from a kind of stone thought to speed up the decomposition of the flesh of corpses; sarcophagus also means 'carnivorous'. When dessert – "grapes, peaches and fresh figs" (p. 59) – is served, one of the guests quotes from *The Fourth Book of Moses*: "And they came onto the brook of Eshcol, and cut down a branch with one cluster of grapes. And they bare it two upon a staff . . . " (p. 59) which goes on: "and they brought of the pomegranates and of the figs."[65] The number twelve is again in evidence, as Babette's guest is referring to, and thereby identifying with, one of the twelve men who the Lord sends to spy out the land of Canaan, which he has promised to the Israelites. The land flows with milk and honey, and they take proof of this fertility home from the vale of Eshcol. Babette's guest is thinking in biblical imagery, but it is now the images of lushness and fertility that impose themselves. Also brought to mind are the fig leaves that were Adam and Eve's visible proof of the Fall, which revealed sexuality and the earthly and mortal life. And in *The New Testament* the fig tree is used in a parable about wishes and fulfilment. Jesus has directed a fig tree to wither, which it duly does, whereupon Peter asks for an explanation, which is as follows: "For verily I say unto you, That whosoever shall say unto this mountain, Be thou removed, and be thou cast into the sea; and shall not doubt in his heart, but shall believe that those things which he saith shall come to pass; he shall have whatsoever he saith. Therefore I say unto you, What things soever ye desire, when ye pray, believe that ye receive them, and ye shall have them."[66] In "The Diver" Saufe has a comment which is virtually a supplement to Jesus' words: "Until this day . . . nobody has seen the trekking-birds take their way toward such warmer spheres as do not exist, or the rivers break their course through rocks and plains to run into an ocean which is not to be found. For God does not create a longing or a hope without having a fulfilling reality ready for them. But our longing is our pledge,"[67] and Thorkild Bjørnvig quotes Karen Blixen as having said: "Longing itself is a pledge that what we long for exists."[68] Babette's dinner redeems a pledge of this nature; the accomplishment of something she has longed for during the course of twelve years and has known existed. By exercising all the gifts and potential that she embodies in the creation of the dinner, she once again realises her destiny. At the same time, the dinner is a revelation of what the guests have longed for, but which they thought did not exist; they are presented with what they have missed out on by not pursuing what they have longed for – and this longing was the pledge guaranteeing that it *did* exist. Babette performs and serves the very best, therefore the guests are offered *Veuve Cliquot 1860*, which bears the name of Madame Cliquot, who ran her champagne production under the motto: "Only one quality – the best." For the first time in their lives the guests deny themselves nothing, and they experience "the intoxication brought about by the noblest wine of the world" (p. 59).

This intoxication is an expression of the fact that the guests disconnect from restrictions and surrender themselves to spontaneity. They never usually spoke very much at mealtimes – what did they have to recount? – but now tongues are loosened, and if they previously felt "a little heavy" they now grow "lighter of heart" (p. 57). Melancholy, which in Kierkegaard's terminology is an expression of the sinful lack of self-realisation, loses ground as the repressed come to self-expression. The guests leave their senses – "beyond comprehension" (p. 66) – and allow themselves to be led by their unconscious minds; they have difficulty in remembering what happened in the course of that evening: "None of the guests later on had any clear remembrance of it" (p. 61) and "try as they might, they could not themselves remember any of the dishes which had been served" (p. 64). At the same time, this failure of memory can be seen as the displacement that is (again) activated after the dinner, as Babette's meal is strong meat when they recover their 'senses'. Babette serves up all the pleasure they have hitherto renounced, but subconsciously longed for. It is highly ironic that renunciation has brought about "discord and dissension" (p. 38) in the Dean's flock, whereas the stimulus of the dinner makes them blissful and amenable. Thus two old women are reconciled – but this is after they have been on bad terms all their adult lives, referred to as "the evil period in which they had been stuck" (p. 61). Their offences against one another stem from the holy renunciation, and instead of the love of one's neighbour, which should be the outcome, we find – in the Danish writer Johannes Møllehave's words – "the repressed desire turned into aggression and hatred and rancour".[69]

The inactive and self-denying life they have led since early youth is lifted from their shoulders by Babette. They are like children again, frisky and without the burdensome guilt which adult life brings with it: "In the street the snow was lying so deep that it had become difficult to walk. The guests from the yellow house wavered on their feet, staggered, sat down abruptly or fell forward on their knees and hands and were covered with snow, as if they had indeed had their sins washed white as wool, and in this regained innocent attire were gamboling like little lambs. It was, to each of them, blissful to have become as a small child" (p. 63). The Brothers and Sisters blossom as children free of restrictive common sense; they come right down to earth, on all fours, like little infants – and even like baby lambs with genuine untamed energy.

The sin from which they are thereby released is indicated with an ironic reference to *The Book of Isaiah* in which we read: "Come now, and let us reason together, saith the Lord: though your sins be as scarlet, they shall be as white as snow; though they be red like crimson, they shall be as wool."[70] In "Babette's Feast", on the other hand, they are released from the sin into which they have been led by the Bible's whitewashing – the sin leaves them when they are taken in the completely opposite direction, this being the scope facilitated by virtue of Babette's black magic. If the Brothers and Sisters have hitherto lived as "the great white flock, we see / as a thousand mountains full of snow", which in the Danish pietist poet Hans Adolf Brorson's hymn[71] is the crowd living in the heavenly, far removed from the "great tribulation", they are now under the influence of Babette's feast – right down on the

Karen Blixen: Young woman with high-necked blouse
Pencil and charcoal on paper, 41 × 36 cm, 1904–6,
The Karen Blixen Museum
Photograph: Jacob Skov-Hansen

Karen Blixen: Young girl, profile
Pencil and charcoal on yellow paper, 61 × 47.5 cm, pre-1914,
The Royal Library, Copenhagen
Photograph: Ole Woldbye

earth, crawling in the black world; but it is only once they are here that they can feel free and absolved.

"Babette's Feast" and "The Dead"

Babette turns the snow into a terrestrial substance. Prior to the dinner the snow belongs in a Brorsonesque Paradise. Martine and Philippa have a beauty of "almost supernatural fairness" with the quality of "perpetual snow" (p. 24), and in his letter Papin calls Philippa "my lost Zerlina" who will therefore forever be "soprano of the snow", and so she will only "enchant the angels" (p. 34). In contrast, Babette's art is the delicious morsel that is tangible and immediate and can trigger off a snow storm, making earth and heaven merge into one. This is a completely new experience for the sisters and the congregation: "such a heavy snowfall had never been known in Berlevaag" (p. 63). With Babette's dinner, the snow becomes an element in which the Brothers and Sisters can veritably roll – on the earth. The snow loses its quality of perpetuity and becomes a terrestrial delight, but the earthly is also transitory – as written in the wake of vain Loewenhielm, who arrives at the house in Berlevaag in a sledge: "Large snowflakes fell densely; behind the sledge the tracks were wiped out quickly" (p. 54).

The definitive death, which both intensifies and wipes out human aspiration, is also to be found in James Joyce's story "The Dead",[72] which has so many points of resemblance to "Babette's Feast" that it is quite conceivable it inspired Karen Blixen. In "The Dead" we meet two elderly sisters who have lived together all their lives; they took in their niece when she was a little girl and have kept her in their own state of spinsterhood and virginity. The niece now keeps house for the three of them. Like Philippa, one of the sisters, Julia, had the potential to be a great singer 30 years ago, but she is said to have wasted her voice in the church choir. The lifelessness we see in Martine and Philippa recurs with Julia and her sister, who are indeed "the dead". The central event in "The Dead" is a dinner party held by the sisters, and which is no less lavish than Babette's feast and described in just as much detail. Julia sings for them all before the dinner, and afterwards Mr D'Arcy, whose voice has developed into that of a true tenor, also performs. A central topic of conversation is the art of opera before and now, the guests lamenting lost glory and calling to mind "how the gallery boys would sometimes in their enthusiasm unyoke the horses from the carriage of some great *prima donna* and pull her themselves through the streets to her hotel."[73] The prima donna could have been Julia, and when Karen Blixen lets Papin hold out the same prospect to Philippa, she makes use of the image from "The Dead": "When she left the Grand Opera upon her master's arm, the crowd would unharness her horses, and themselves draw her to the Café Anglais . . . " (pp. 30–1)!

A high-point during the dinner in "The Dead" comes when Gabriel Conroy, the sisters' nephew, makes a speech to the hostesses. Like Loewenhielm, Gabriel comes from a "great world outside", and he is a university lecturer "orating to vulgarians".[74] The dinner triggers off a snowstorm the like of which has not been seen for 30 years, and here too the sky is pulled down to earth: "the sky seemed to be descending."[75] When Gabriel and his wife Gretta have returned by horse-drawn carriage through the snow to their hotel, Gabriel learns that a song heard during the course of the party had reminded her of a sweetheart, Michael Furey, who had died for her sake when she was young. Michael, who also had a good voice, had sung the same song for her. Gabriel, with a conceited hope, takes Gretta's outburst on account of the song to be desire directed towards himself. Michael's uncompromising action and the love between him and Gretta comes between Gabriel and Gretta, just as Gabriel has fallen in love with her all over again and is about to seduce her. At one and the same time, Michael's death symbolises true and intense love, loss of illusions and death that will separate everyone. After Gretta has fallen asleep, Gabriel becomes aware of the passing of her facial beauty, and he thinks of one of his aunts soon to die, and finally looks out at the snow which symbolises mortality: "It was falling, too, upon every part of the lonely churchyard on the hill where Michael Furey lay buried. It lay thickly drifted on the crooked crosses and head-stones, on the spears of the little gate, on the barren thorns. His soul swooned slowly as he heard the snow falling faintly through the universe and faintly falling, like the descent of their last end, upon all the living and the dead."[76]

Vanity and mortality: Loewenhielm

When Lorens Loewenhielm comes to Berlevaag for the first time, it is as punishment for his merry and dissolute life, which has lead him into debt. His father has sent him into exile so that he will be able "to meditate and to better his ways" (p. 25). The opportunity with which he is confronted in the person of Martine is that of a 'pure' life: a "mighty vision of a higher and purer life ... " (p. 26). Loewenhielm falls in love with "a gentle, golden-haired angel" (p. 26) who has not been brought up to a life in the earthly sense that Loewenhielm cannot relinquish – as when the Dean rattles off a quotation from the Bible at the dinner table, and Loewenhielm can only think in worldly terms: "'Mercy and Truth, dear brethren, have met together,' said the Dean. 'Righteousness and Bliss have kissed one another.' And the young man's thoughts were with the moment when Lorens and Martine should be kissing each other" (p. 26).[77] Loewenhielm – unlike Papin, who kisses Philippa – never gets around to kissing Martine, but even if he had, it would have turned out the same for him as for Papin, as the sisters are unable to reciprocate earthly love. There is a gulf between them; Loewenhielm "could find nothing at all to say" (p. 26) and cannot tell her how he feels – which shows his lack of courage, but more particularly the simple fact that there would be no understanding and response on her part.

Life in the Dean's house robs Loewenhielm of the drive which he had not previously lacked in relation to girls, and he cannot realise the dream of Martine; fundamentally this is because Martine is indeed an unrealistic dream: "Was it the family madness which made him still carry with him the dream-like picture of a maiden so fair that she made the air around her shine with purity and holiness? He did not want to be a dreamer; he wanted to be like his brother-officers" (p. 27). Therefore, it is not just banter, but also an accurate analysis, when his fellow officers consider Loewenhielm's love affair in Berlevaag to be "a pitiful business" (p. 27). Loewenhielm's parting words to Martine – "I have learned here that Fate is hard, and that in this world there are things which are impossible!" (p. 27) – are quite right inasmuch as the 'pure' life, which Martine represents, is indeed impossible.

The restricted and lifeless world into which Loewenhielm and Papin step is again expressed in the small/large symbolism, as both of them shrink – like Babette – during their stay in Berlevaag; of Loewenhielm it is said: "He repeated his visit time after time, and each time seemed to himself to grow smaller and more insignificant and contemptible" (p. 26), and Papin "felt small in the sublime surroundings ... " (p. 29).

In the person of Martine, Loewenhielm might have found an ideal, but it is an unrealistic one, because she lacks the other side of life, the earthly and sensual. She is therefore unrealisable, but the outcome of his encounter with her is nevertheless that Loewenhielm pulls himself together and single-mindedly concentrates on his military career. From the "perpetual snow" he is thrown back upon this world, and adapts himself accordingly, but he is still able to exploit the ideals and does so at Court, being liberal with the Bible quotations he has heard in the Dean's house, which helps his career as "piety was now in fashion at Court" (p. 28) – the use of "now" revealing that Loewenhielm has learned to play the game with its successes and costs. Occasionally in the course of his career, Loewenhielm suffers from a "fear of a dream" (not in the English-language version, p. 36 in the Danish version), which shows both the price he pays and the regression to pure madness he fears.

The runner tracks, which are wiped out by the falling snow as Loewenhielm is again on his way to Berlevaag after 29 years away, are a stark comment on the thorn that is tormenting him as he rides in the sledge: he finds himself "worrying about his immortal soul" (p. 52). Loewenhielm fears that his responsible and extremely busy existence – which has led to a glorious military career, secured status at Court, a large circle of friends and an immaculate home life – has repressed his dreams and fancies and robbed him of eternal life. As he is now "tired of the great world" (not in the English-language version, p. 55 in the Danish version), he experiences a compelling need for these aspects of life as well – what he has lacked and fears never to share – which he hides behind the question of whether or not he was right as a young man to leave Martine.

There is a difference between how Loewenhielm saw Martine when he was a young man and the significance he ascribes to her as an older, tired man. Martine is sited, as it were, before everything gets going for Loewenhielm and after he has achieved everything he can on the path in life he chose. But there is an extra difference at the latter meeting: Babette. Loewenhielm looks back over the past 29 years during which so much has happened for him, but nothing for Martine. He is aware that as a young man he "had felt himself to be a shy and sorry figure in the house of the Dean" (p. 53) and that therefore he "had shaken its dust off his riding boots" (s. 53). Now the sisters' "low rooms, the haddock and the glass of water on the table" (p. 53) will definitively convince him that "in their milieu the existence of Lorens Loewenhielm would very soon have become sheer misery" (p. 53). The irony is that it would indeed have proven such had Babette not been there to cause Loewenhielm the great surprise, leaving him totally bewildered. Thus he makes the same mistake as Papin, who in his letter believes Philippa to be surrounded by a large family and thereby in bountiful circumstances – leading Papin to conclude that Philippa made the better choice than he, who was famous, but later became "gray, lonely, forgotten" (p. 34); like Loewenhielm, Papin is preoccupied with death. At Babette's dinner, Loewenhielm is the only one who knows what he is eating, because he has eaten Babette's dishes in Paris, but he does not discover that she is also responsible for the dinner in Berlevaag. He cannot do otherwise than ascribe it to the sisters, and by so doing he is caught in a net that displays his 'external' life, lacking inner life and spirituality. That the sisters' home is the one place in the world in which Loewenhielm would least expect to be served a meal à la Babette also makes the simple point that the divine does not have to be sought in heaven or in far-removed places, but that it is to be found here and now and just around the corner.

Loewenhielm is vainly anxious about his immortal soul, and now he also wants to have a share in eternal life in the same way that he has taken part in the earthly. An amusing manifestation of this is Loewenhielm's egoistic endeavour to dominate the conversation – the 'spirit' – in the home where, as a young man, he had been obliged to sit in silence. Here he resorts – again – to tricks from the world in which he has had so much success. First, he flatters the sisters and the congregation by telling them that the Dean's collection of sermons was one of the Queen's favourite books – thus also drawing attention to the very person who had recommended this collection to Her Majesty. He then – intoxicated by the wine and transported by the meal, which he thinks has been prepared in the spirit of the sisters – makes a speech which is one long quotation from the Dean. He achieves the same success as when he enraptured the Court with the Dean's words. Loewenhielm now dominates the Dean's home, and his sermon about choice and grace is grist to his and his audience's mill:

> *"'Mercy and truth, my friends, have met together,' said the General. 'Righteousness and bliss shall kiss one another . . . Man, my friends,' said General Loewenhielm, 'is frail and foolish. We have all of us been told that grace is to be found in the universe. But in our human foolishness and short-sightedness we imagine divine grace to be finite . . . We tremble before making our choice in life, and after having made it again tremble in fear of having chosen wrong. But the moment comes when our eyes are opened, and we see and realize that grace is infinite. Grace, my friends, demands nothing from us but that we shall await it with confidence and acknowledge it in gratitude. Grace, brothers, makes no conditions and singles out none of us in particular; grace takes us all to its bosom and proclaims general amnesty. See! that which we have chosen is given us, and that which we have refused is, also and at the same time, granted us.*

Ay, that which we have rejected is poured upon us abundantly. For mercy and truth have met together, and righteousness and bliss have kissed one another!'" (pp. 59–61)

Like a saviour, Loewenhielm grants himself all eternity and everything that, through his choices in life, he has ruled out. The sisters and the congregation are given that which, through their passivity, they have never lifted a finger to share in. Loewenhielm acts as stand-in for the Dean, he is "but a mouthpiece for a message which meant to be brought forth" (p. 60). He dominates the home because "the sound of well-known and cherished words had seized and moved" (p. 61) the sisters and the congregation, and therefore Martine is also able to call Loewenhielm "dear brother" (p. 63) just before they part. With Loewenhielm's speech about grace, they can all disclaim responsibility for the actions or lack of them which have characterised their lives.

But there is doubleness in Loewenhielm's speech, which makes him the mouthpiece for another message too – the one to be found in Babette's dinner: the feast is in itself a demonstration of everything the twelve people at the table have lacked and which Babette now 'serves' them, but the connection never dawns on them. Loewenhielm shares in that inner life and spirituality which he has missed; the sisters and congregation experience the earthly and bodily which they have despised, but they appreciate the experience purely as a manifestation of God's grace and thereby maintain the separation, whereas Babette's grace is found in the union of the parts. The twofold nature of the message becomes clear when Martine and Loewenhielm agree that "in this world anything is possible" (p. 62), which is indeed the essence of Babette's message, but Martine's and Loewenhielm's premise for their agreement is that they will henceforth be united "if not in the flesh, which means nothing, in spirit, which is all" (p. 62) – which in Babette's terms is a woeful premise. That which was impossible for Loewenhielm when he worshipped Martine as a young man, does not become possible until he renounces the flesh. At that time they could not talk with one another, now they can, because conversation takes place on Martine's premises, which the young Lorens had no use for, but which the older eternity-craving Loewenhielm embraces. The twelve at the table experience for a while the liberation and absolution of living an undivided life, but the tragedy is that they are at no point aware of it – which would probably be too much to expect anyway. The reader, however, is permitted to see the wider connection and the twofold message.

The reckoning

Babette's art prevails, which, considering the difficult circumstances, is a triumph, but there is no obvious long-term prospect for her art as no understanding whatsoever is generated in the sisters. The final scene, a conversation in the kitchen between the sisters and Babette after everyone else has left, is a formidable, condensed highlighting of this tragic outcome to the story. Babette stands her ground in the kitchen at Berlevaag just as heroically as when she stood on the barricades in Paris, but the outcome for both confrontations is that the system waged against remains in control at the end.

Robert Langbaum has reached a completely opposite interpretation, concluding "the story ends well with Philippa's fulfillment, matching Martine's. Philippa's understanding grows along with a growing tenderness for Babette."[78] But to this should be added that, to the end, Babette emphasises how "little" the sisters are, and the tenderness as mentioned in the opening remark of the final scene more than intimates that this tenderness should not be taken at face value: "When Martine and Philippa locked the door they remembered Babette. A little wave of tenderness and pity swept through them: Babette alone had had no share in the bliss of the evening" (p. 64). One has to ask Langbaum how the sisters can be understanding when they only remember Babette after the guests have left, and when they cannot see that she is responsible for the "bliss".

In "Babette's Feast", tenderness and pity as manifest in the sisters is subject to a critique of an acuteness and extent reminiscent of Nietzsche:

> "*Christianity is called the religion of* pity . . . *Schopenhauer was consistent enough: pity negates life and renders it* more deserving of negation.
>
> *Pity is the practice of nihilism. To repeat: this depressive and contagious instinct crosses those instincts which aim at the preservation of life and at the enhancement of its value . . . pity persuades men to* nothingness! *Of course, one does not say 'nothingness' but 'beyond' or 'God', or 'true life', or Nirvana, salvation, blessedness.*
>
> *This innocent rhetoric from the realm of the religious—moral idiosyncrasy appears much less innocent as soon as we realize which tendency it is that here shrouds itself in sublime words:* hostility *against life. Schopenhauer was hostile to life; therefore pity became a virtue for him.*"[79]

Martine and Philippa almost smother Babette's self-expression in sympathy; they exclaim: "Oh, my poor Babette" (p. 65), but this utterance is turned around a little later when Babette refers to Philippa as "my poor lady" (p. 68). The sisters' religious perspective limits them to seeing Babette's achievement as "an unforgettable proof of human loyalty and self-sacrifice" (p. 66), but the case is quite the opposite, as is clearly apparent when Babette meets the sisters' comment "you ought not to have given away all you had for our sake" (p. 66) with a glance which had "even scorn, at the bottom of it" (p. 66) and with a wholly admonishing retort: "'For your sake?' she replied. 'No. For my own.'" (p. 66). Emphasising the import of Babette's reply, we immediately learn that she "looks unaccustomedly big" and spoke with words of "the same stature" (not in the English-language version, p. 72 in the Danish version). The sisters do not have the imagination to envisage that one can do something for one's own sake; the exchange of views is in every particular a striking exposure of the self-denying outlook on life by means of which they have made themselves guilty, not just in relation to their own lives, but also in relation to Babette – the exchange being of course two sides of the same issue.

The violent confrontation of the final scene is particularised in a war metaphor: "Babette's eyes met Philippa's like a pair of heavy canons drawn into position" (not in the English-language version, p. 73 in the Danish version), with Philippa, who sets aside *her own* talents as an artist, the target. The Communard and freedom fighter from Paris is inseparable from the rebel in Berlevaag; now the gunpowder burns come from the "black and greasy pots and pans" (p. 64) which surround Babette as she sits exhausted – a similar state as after the uprising in Paris.

Babette stakes everything she owns – the ten thousand francs – on her dinner; she gives herself completely for her art, but it is categorically stated that for the sisters this act was "incomprehensible to them" (p. 66). They do not understand even the most elementary intention of the dinner – which can be added to the discrepancy with Langbaum's analysis of the sisters' insight and understanding as the story's happy ending. The sisters grasp at an outlandish comparison in order to explain (away) the event, in that Martine likens Babette to an African chief who in gratitude to a white Christian medicine man – here with a little good will one can see Babette contra the Dean – serves up his baby grandchild as a rich meal, and Martine concludes: "Babette became completely dark in Martine's eyes, just as wild as the old

African chief. In the course of a few hours she had let the good Christians of Berlevaag unwittingly devour a human foothold in life and refuge in old age. She shuddered and folded her hands together" (not in the English-language version, p. 72 in the Danish version). To Martine the dinner represents a loss of security and immunity, the elements in which *she* wraps herself, and therefore she clasps her hands in prayer. The darkness and wildness is Martine's way of excluding Babette, but on the story's deeper level it is an expression of the original, genuine and natural character of Babette. And the offering of the child – the future – is the ultimate expression of Babette's uncompromising approach: she is prepared to stake her life for her art.

But the offering of the child is also a metaphor for Babette's patent lack of a future. She will not return to Paris, for the aristocrats – who, in contrast to the sisters, understood and appreciated her art – are no longer there, and *they* had such high regard for her art that they would readily have offered *their* lives for her. Even though Babette fought against the aristocracy as oppressors of the people, they were on the same side when it came to great and genuine art, but the aristocracy as Babette's allies in terms of art should, at a deeper level, be read as a definition of Babette's art as aristocratic in the best Karen Blixen sense of the word. The fact that Babette remains in Berlevaag thus also demonstrates that there is no longer scope for aristocratic art, and no longer connoisseurs and devotees of this great art. Babette could make the aristocrats "perfectly happy" (p. 68) when she did her very best, and furthermore she tells the sisters that Papin had explained to her how terrible it is for artists not to do their best; here Papin has undoubtedly had his Philippa in mind, and it can be added: how dreadful it must have been for Babette to spend twelve years "doing" at the bottom of the scale in Berlevaag! Babette can triumphantly tell the sisters: "I am a great artist!" (p. 66), for in her dinner she has realised Papin's words to her that: "Through all the world there goes one long cry from the heart of the artist: Give me leave to do my utmost!" (p. 68). Even if it is for the last time, Babette has yet again exercised all her incarnate talents, by means of which she has brought herself into the three kinds of perfect happiness which Yorick proposes in Karen Blixen's tale "Converse at Night in Copenhagen": "to feel in oneself an excess of strength"; "to know for certain that you are fulfilling the will of God"(to accomplish one's God-given destiny); and "the cessation of pain."[80]

Eventually, after the dinner, Babette tells the sisters that she was once cook at the Café Anglais and on learning this "deep, forgotten chords vibrated" (p. 67) in Philippa's heart. In his letter Papin lamented that Philippa had never had the opportunity to sing at the Grand Opera of Paris, and thus never became the great artist "that God meant you to be" (p. 34). In contrast to Babette, Philippa does not accomplish her destiny, and Papin's solace — that she will sing in Paradise instead — is in reality a deep sorrow about an irredeemably wasted talent. It is therefore tragic that the final words of the story are Philippa's repetition of Papin's words to her, which she now addresses to Babette: "Yet this is not the end! I feel, Babette, that this is not the end. In Paradise you will be the great artist that God meant you to be! . . . Ah, how you will enchant the angels!" (p. 68). It is an insult to console Babette in this way, considering that Philippa has experienced her great art at first hand, and, moreover, Babette has just explained that she has thus demonstrated that she *is* a great artist. The episode confirms that Philippa has understood nothing. In a certain sense Papin's words are still directed towards her, and at the same time they express those aspects of Philippa that are personified by Babette — which provides another explanation for Babette remaining in service in Berlevaag. No liberation has taken place in Philippa, and, as Babette can also be seen as the oppressed part of Philippa, Babette has to remain oppressed in Berlevaag. In Philippa's response — that Babette will enchant the angels — there is, furthermore, a dire affirmation that Babette will continue to be a serving spirit in Philippa and Martine's Paradise. Just before Philippa's concluding words, we are told with unfailing emphasis: "Philippa went up to Babette and put her arms round her. She felt the cook's body like a marble monument against her own" (p. 68) — Babette has erected a monument to the great art which she embodies, but at the same time it has the significance of a memorial as she is like a statue in Philippa's embrace.

Babette and Pellegrina

In "The Dreamers" from *Seven Gothic Tales*, Pellegrina Leoni is adored by grand and poor alike for her great talent as an opera singer, but when she loses her voice she becomes a dangerous revolutionary and her house a veritable witches' cauldron. Babette has a forerunner in Pellegrina, but also a successor as Pellegrina appears again in "Echoes" from *Last Tales*. In "Echoes" there is clear resonance from "Babette's Feast", which underlines Babette's and Papin's unsuccessful attempts to open Berlevaag up to the world of art and love.

Just like Babette and Papin, Pellegrina in "Echoes" comes from the great outside to a small mountain town which seems to be "relinquishing the world".[81] Pellegrina is also desolate and an exile with a lost singing voice, but, like Papin, she comes back to life again when she hears a peasant boy singing in church. She undertakes to give this boy, Emanuele, singing lessons. In more or less the same words as Papin uses to Philippa, Pellegrina describes to Emanuele the worldly splendour awaiting him as a great singer: he would be beloved by the mighty of the earth, and the audience would unspan the horses from his coach and pull it themselves in a triumphal procession through the town. But Emanuele is paralysed by growing up in the mountain town, the surrounding wall restricting his horizon, and as Babette turns to stone in Philippa's embrace, so Emanuele's response is to throw stones at Pellegrina and accuse her of being both a witch and a vampire. Babette's eyes flash like canons in the final confrontation, and Pellegrina's attack on Emanuele is no less forceful: "But what are you, who dare not come down to play with a witch? What is a coward's soul worth? Must you sit on that soul of yours as a young miss on her maidenhood ... you are being poisoned by your soul."[82] Pellegrina laments that Emanuele squanders his talent as the village saint he becomes, but it is stated quite plainly that his destiny is also the consequence of an environment in which everyone is "strained and anxious".[83] In such an environment, the joy offered by Pellegrina falls on poor soil: "Joy may come to them ... as a surprise, for an hour or two, but none of them feels at home in it."[84] A better description could not be given of the Brothers' and Sisters' experience of Babette's dinner, the joy of which has no lasting effect in Berlevaag either.

III Liberation of Destiny – "The Ring"

Outline

The short, dense tale "The Ring" rounds off *Anecdotes of Destiny*, but with the leading character Lise's independent step out into freedom "The Ring" is also an opening for new tales. Lise takes in hand the problems that remain hard and fast for Martine and Philippa in "Babette's Feast". These two tales in particular supplement one another, but "The Ring" differs from the other stories in *Anecdotes of Destiny* in one important respect: it is the only tale in which art is not seen in relation to the life being described. "The Ring" was published in 1950, and in the following year Karen Blixen told the story on Danish radio, and included it in the selection from her writings *Fra det gamle Danmark 1–2* (*Old Danish Tales 1–2*, 1963), which was ready for publication shortly before her death.

"The Ring" takes place on "a summer morning a hundred and fifty years ago" (p. 221), more precisely a morning in July, but the year is not specified. If, however, we assume that the narrator tells the tale in retrospect from the year in which the book was written, as seen in "Babette's Feast", then the narrator of "The Ring" is telling the story in 1950, and thus the tale takes place in 1800, which would tally with the milieu descriptions.

Nineteen-year-old Lovisa, called Lise, and 24-year-old squire Sigismund have been married for a week. Even though their love goes right back to their childhood, they have met with constant opposition from Lise's noble and wealthier family, who cannot accept Sigismund's ancestry in the lesser nobility. Their relationship, however, has flourished so strongly undercover that Lise's parents have had to give in, and now the newly-weds can display their love openly – openness is also the clear resolve of them both: Sigismund will not allow a shadow to fall across his bride's path, and Lise will have no secrets from her husband. Consequently, their life is still a state of paradise with "jesting and railleries" (p. 235) and without sensual, earthly love. Sigismund is called a baby, and Lise is all white innocence, although she has thoughts that make her blush. When she and Sigismund are out on the estate inspecting some sick lambs and the sheepmaster tells them about a violent sheep thief, she is quite fascinated, even though outwardly she expresses distaste. Sigismund displays understanding of the sheep thief and impatiently sends Lise home alone, which delights her. She wanders from the direct route and walks into a hidden, secret place in the grove. This is a movement from the white into the dark, a warning sign of the sheep thief that she meets there. The encounter could mean death for both of them, but it takes place under the sign of metamorphosis and evolution, in that Lise stakes her wedding ring. She enters a new union – with the sheep thief – and when she leaves him she has stepped out of the state of paradise. A shadow has been cast across Lise, and Sigismund is subjected to her secretiveness when he catches her up. He cannot get an answer to his question about where she lost the ring.

On the threshold

With the happy wedding, "The Ring" starts where many romantic stories end: "they would walk and drive so till the end of their days. Their distant paradise had descended to earth" (p. 235), where it should however be noted that the reference to the earth also gives notice of the approaching realities. Marriage and the new rural surroundings give Lise a feeling of freedom she has never experienced before, but the innocence and ignorance in which her childhood home has kept her has yet to be breached. Therefore she is enveloped in white: when she goes out white woolly clouds drift above her, she is wearing "a white muslin frock" (p. 236), and passion is reserved for her white lapdog Bijou, whose French name has the pertinent figurative meaning 'apple of one's eye'. It is stated quite plainly that here we have a 19-year-old who has only just left her doll's house and is still living in its concept universe: "It was not a long time since she had played with dolls; as now she dressed her own hair, looked over her linen press and arranged her flowers she again lived through an enchanting and cherished experience: one was doing everything gravely and solicitously, and all the time one knew one was playing" (pp. 235–6). The description of Lise is reminiscent of Martine and Philippa in their youth, but whereas they remain in the doll's house, she steps out of it. The significance of the word "own" in the above passage reveals that a change has taken place: Lise must now do for herself what others in her childhood home did for her or instructed her to do – intimate, personal things, which attest to the overprotective environment from which she comes.

Sigismund is concerned about Lise being able to come to terms with her new life – understood by Lise as his fear that his life is not good enough for her, but Sigismund has good reason to have her childhood ivory tower in his worried mind. Despite the idyll, or rather because of the unreal in the idyllic marriage, there is a distance between the couple. Lise also exhibits impatience. When, earlier in the week, Sigismund had wanted to take her out for a ride, she had not wanted to go with him, and now, as he explains the possibilities and difficulties in breeding sheep, she thinks: "'How clever he is, what a lot of things he knows!' and at the same time: 'What an absurd person he is, with his sheep! What a baby he is!'" (p. 236). Her need to be alone is an expression of something missing in their relationship – among other things, the longing for independence that is apparent in Lise's craving for solitude.

Lise's emphasis on Sigismund being clever and knowledgeable implies, moreover, the interplay of the masculine and the feminine that is often present in Karen Blixen's work. Lise's words imply that Sigismund is governed by logic and facts and thereby suppresses the feminine and thus his development to adulthood, whereas Sigismund's impatience with Lise is due to the fact that she lives in an unrealistic dreamworld with no contact with the masculine, which here is the reality that can put her dreams on firm ground. Lise and Sigismund regard one another as immature, because their relationship lacks the balance between the feminine and the masculine, but the prerequisite for this to emerge is that they each become whole personalities – and here we have the old story about resolving the schism between dream and reality, emotion and intellect. For Karen Blixen it is also a question of uniting eternity and time: in *Karen Blixen in Denmark: Letters, 1931–62* she describes the feminine as the state of *being* and says that the woman belongs "to eternity",[85] whereas the masculine is to be found in action and achievement, which is linked to the passage of time. To Karen Blixen, the masculine and the feminine are not only a question of the two genders, but also exist side by side in every person irrespective of gender. As such, "The Ring" is a story about a relationship between two people and about the resources necessary within the individual to accomplish the development to adulthood. That Lise and Sigismund's relationship can be traced right back to their childhood implies that they can be seen as one person.

Lise and Sigismund share an instinct to achieve these conditions, and both of them have to adjust. Sigismund is undoubtedly not satisfied with the white innocence he has married, but he is not actually antagonistic to her. Leif Søndergaard is of the opinion that in her encounter with the sheep thief, Lise commits a necessary adultery, because it is only by this means that she can become a woman, and that the fundamental cause is Sigismund's role as a traditional husband who is merely a new father figure for Lise and does not understand her needs as a woman: "Sigismund is incapable of meeting her erotic forces. At no point does he understand what is stirring in Lise, but is only concerned about the practical business with his sheep."[86] My point of view is that Lise's upbringing and childhood environment, personified in her "Grandmamma", is the obstacle with which both Lise *and* Sigismund are struggling. "Grandmamma" has the same status as the father, the Dean, in "Babette's Feast". Leif Søndergaard further claims that "Sigismund keeps her arrested in childhood"[87] and that he is therefore not himself equipped to step into the adult world. I would suggest that Sigismund and the sheep thief are two sides of the same coin, rather than playing the roles of respectively husband and marriage wrecker that Leif Søndergaard gives them. It is true that the sheep thief contributes to breaking down Lise's conventional and childish perception of marriage, but this could also be in Sigismund's interest. Moreover, there is the point that the sheep thief also receives something developmental from his encounter with Lise, and this – in as much as the sheep thief is seen as a side of Sigismund – means something developmental for Sigismund's process of maturity.

Sigismund does not actually regard the sheep thief as a rival. On the contrary, it is after he has been fully informed about the sheep thief's wolf-like nature that he sends Lise home alone – knowing quite well that the sheep thief is still in the vicinity. He is well aware that Lise might meet the sheep thief, and actually sends her off into the arms of the one who teaches her about the harsh and carnal realities of life. Just before this happens, he voices pity for the sheep thief by exclaiming: "Poor devil" (p. 238). In other words, he has shown sympathy with the demonic, and in this he is in opposition to "Grandmamma" and the influence she has over Lise. Lise, who has also been intensely affected and fascinated by the sheepmaster's account of the sheep thief, reacts to Sigismund's defence of the devil with a regression to Grandmamma's world picture: "Lise said: 'How can you pity such a terrible man? Indeed Grandmamma was right when she said that you were a revolutionary and a danger to society!' The thought of Grandmamma, and of the tears of past days, again turned her mind away from the gruesome tale she had just heard" (p. 238). It is difficult to see Sigismund as a new 'father-figure' for Lise, when it is here so clearly stated why Lise's family has objected to him as Lise's husband. In Grandmamma's eyes, Sigismund is a free-thinker and thus a danger to the established order that she repre-sents – as indeed is the sheep thief. A simple phrase in this passage is of great significance: "tears of past days", which is a clear indication of the incarceration that was Lise's lot in Grandmamma's world. The passage shows that, at this point, Lise has a foot in both camps; she is on the way to liberation, as heralded by the news about the sheep thief and her reac-tion, but Grandmamma still has the power to keep Lise's thoughts in check to such an extent that she is able to forget the sheep thief and return him to her unconscious mind.

The liberation process is, however, set out in detail: "Twice her own thoughts made her blush deeply and happily" (p. 237). Despite her bond to Grandmamma, Lise manifests independent thought, and her blushes are not accompanied by a sense of shame, but one of happiness. Therefore she is totally engrossed by the sheepmaster's account of the sheep thief, and she even asks to be told it once more. The sheepmaster describes the sheep thief, three times in a row, as a "wolf" who has killed a man in an utterly savage fashion: violent and very bloody. The lack of shame is succeeded by the delight Lise feels when the account of the sheep thief leads her thoughts to the story about Little Red Ridinghood: "She remembered Red Ridinghood's wolf, and felt a pleasant little thrill running down her spine" (p. 237). Although the recollection of this fairy tale also demonstrates Lise's bond to the 'childish' world picture, it is fundamentally the 'adult' symbolism of the fairy tale that stirs Lise. It is evident that Lise sees herself, the sheep thief and Grandmamma reflected in Little Red Ridinghood, the wolf and the grandmother. In the fairy tale Red Ridinghood shows the wolf the way to grandmother; the wolf tells Ridinghood that she only thinks about her duties and is therefore unable to appreciate the beauty of 'the forest'; the wolf then makes Red Ridinghood go into the depths of the forest, while he goes and devours the grandmother. The wolf gains access to the grandmother's house by pretending to be Red Ridinghood; dressed in the grandmother's clothes, the wolf devours Red Ridinghood.[88] Through the 'duties' that she has had in relation to Grandmamma, Lise is able to rediscover that which has prevented her from going 'wild'; the wolf concealed inside the kindly grandmother is here an expression of the evil caused by Grandmamma's shield – which could be the undoing of Lise. But Lise's delight at the thought of the fairy tale shows a desire to challenge this situation: to ally herself with the sheep thief, so that he can dispose of – devour – what Grandmamma represents, and thereafter 'eat' Lise – with the forthright desire for sensual gratification which this implies.

Marriage in the forest

For Lise, nothing could be sweeter than to be sent home alone by Sigismund – the consequence of their shared knowledge about the sheep thief waiting in the darkness. In response to Sigismund's request that she start walking home, she takes off her summer hat, thus complying with Sigismund's intention. In the fairy tale, Red Ridinghood is not frightened when she meets the wolf for the first time, for she is not aware of its true nature, but Lise goes dauntlessly off to face the sheep thief, even though she is acquainted with his nature. Under the impact of the report about the sheep thief and the consequent association to the fairy tale about Red Ridinghood, Lise does not take the most *direct* route, but instead goes into the forest; the forest light is elsewhere characterised by Karen Blixen in "The Poet": "The light within, less bright than before, seems more powerful, filled with meaning, pregnant with secrets which are light in themselves, although unknowable to mortals."[89] In the forest, Lise meets that which the glaring white light in Grandmamma's world has prevented her from seeing: she perceives previously unseen sides of herself and makes the acquaintance of the unknowable in life.

Lise's meander into the forest is a happy one: "As she walked she felt a great new happiness in being altogether alone, even without Bijou. She could not remember that she had ever before in all her life been altogether alone" (p. 238). Bijou is not there, as pent up sensuality is released, and the delight in being alone is completely understandable in a person who has never previously had the opportunity for independent action. This blissful solitude is accompanied by a sense of expectant tranquillity: "The landscape around her was still, as if full of promise" (pp. 238-9), and this tranquillity imbues the entire encounter with the sheep thief or "beast, who is the silent pulse in the monster of the world", as we have seen Sophus Claussen express it in the poem "Man" from *Diableries*. Lise now plunges into the "hidden", a term which is used in a multitude of varieties, where it is possible – again in Sophus Claussen's "Man" – to find "the living, which gleamed deep in the foliage". Lise is convinced that the anxiety her disappearance will cause Sigismund will increase his "longing" for her. Lise finds freedom by descending into darkness and experiencing a Fall; it is *not* a movement into an abyss where there is no hope, "nothing but darkness and decline", as her destiny is interpreted in *Diana's Revenge*.[90]

Lise's advance into the forest leads her to an alcove, which is quite straightforwardly called "the shelter" (p. 240). She has been there once before, with Bijou, but in order for Lise to be completely alone, she has to be without the white Bijou. Even her initial movement towards the shelter is described as an attack on the white world: first a twig catches the trimming on her white frock, then "a branch took hold of one of her long golden curls", and as she is about to step into the alcove and has to "divide the foliage", she bends down, and "the hem of her dress caught her foot" (p. 240). The foundation of the white world – protection, innocence and modesty – is being challenged, and it is no coincidence that immediately afterwards the sheep thief is described as physically battered, which here could just as well be said of Lise.

To Lise, in the alcove she would be "hidden from all the world" (p. 239), which would "emphasise the secretness of her course" (p. 240). She is seeking her inviolable inner self and succeeds in so doing, as is apparent at the end of the story when she keeps the existence of this place secret from her husband. In a wider sense, the 'secret' is the encounter with the unknowable and uninterpretable in life, which Grandmamma's rigidly constructed and regulated milieu excluded; where once there were clear-cut opinions, one conviction with which to conform, she now encounters the 'meaningless', which is the guarantee of a free rein. This is the devil's domain, and the sheep thief's gestures are also characterised as "unbelievable" (p. 241). In words that we have seen Karen Blixen use about Muhammad, Lise now observes the mysterious and dangerous forces in life and is thereby subjected to erotic power, which brings latent forces to fruition. 'The secret' is the prerequisite of true love. Karen Blixen might very well have been thinking of Steen Steensen Blicher's short story "Tardy Awakening" (1828), in which the main character, Elise, who represents erotic power, says: "Secrecy . . . is the life-principle of love; without this the myrtle lacks both root and stem."[91] Elise is as one with her "mysterious fate"[92] and thus completely at ease with herself – she possesses an "infernal calm."[93] In the eyes of the society to whose narrow bourgeois morality she is a contrast, she is seen as a vampire and "that serpent" which destroys "an earthly paradise" that "separated heaven and hell".[94] The separation drags representatives of bourgeois morality down into "the flaming chasm",[95] but Elise continues to enjoy "perfect health".[96] Bourgeois morality perishes in narrowness, but the love that Elise represents is eternal and natural.

In "The Ring" we are told numerous times that Lise makes no noise and utters no words, emphasising that she has reached a rapport with the stillness and timelessness of the sheep thief. The narrator finds it necessary to state this quite categorically: "The meeting in the wood from beginning to end passed without a word; what happened could only be rendered by pantomime. To the two actors in the pantomime it was timeless; according to a clock it lasted four minutes" (pp. 240–1). Lise and the sheep thief play out an eternal drama: the Fall, the silent pulse of which they are subject to; they become impersonal entities without individual articulation. 'Pantomime' comes from the Greek, its original meaning being 'that which imitates everything'. Lise and the sheep thief assume mythological form by means of which they are 'dehumanised'.

The myth of the Fall suggests the original state, which we all have in common, and this is also manifested as Lise's encounter with the primordial drives and the primitive inarticulate human: the sheep thief's alcove is described as a "covert" with "gnawed bones" on the ground and the cinders of a "fire" (p. 241) – exactly as Babette was compared with the wild chieftain who was an image of this original state, genuine and natural. In the following passage from *Out of Africa*, stillness is the characteristic of the wild and uncivilised in which Lise is instructed: "No domestic animal can be as still as a wild animal. The civilized people have lost the aptitude of stillness, and must take lessons in silence from the wild before they are accepted by it."[97]

There are very clear similarities between Babette and the sheep thief. Babette arrives blackened by gunpowder from the foul reality of a Paris that soaked her in blood; the sheep thief appears to Lise beaten and ragged: "His face was bruised and scratched, his hands and wrists stained with dark filth" (p. 240). He is "the wild animal at bay" (p. 241); Babette appeared to the sisters "wild-eyed like a hunted animal".[98] As Babette was to the sisters, to Lise the sheep thief is the harsh reality about which she has heard nothing from Grandmamma – the suffering and death that appear when she steps outside her paradise. Death is also the silence through which a universal condition speaks: "The silent, all-embracing genius of consent", as Karen Blixen calls death in "The Great Gesture".[99] Both Babette and the sheep thief are oppressed and represent 'the oppressed', which the sisters remain shielded from, even though Babette reveals it to them by way of her dinner. Lise, on the other hand, goes to meet the sheep thief herself, inquisitive and winning. The sisters meet the devil in Babette's witches' sabbath, and Lise, who has heard the sheep thief referred to as a devil, beholds him as a "forest ghost" (p. 241).

The symbolism leaves no room for doubt that in the depths of the forest Lise encounters sexuality. The secret place also represents intimacy, described as "a small alcove with hangings of thick green and golden brocade" (p. 239) – an overgrown space intended for sleeping in – the entrance to which "became moist" (p. 240). The rags hardly cover the sheep thief's nakedness, which is made all the more potent by his right hand hanging down his side and clasping "the hilt of a knife" (p. 240), and when Lise stands before him her white clothes are already ripped. Gesturing with the knife arouses an animal-like agitation in the sheep thief – "his nostrils distended, the corners of his mouth quivered" (pp. 241–2) – and the climax is reached when he wraps Lise's handkerchief – her hymen (it is also referred to as "cambric", (p. 242)

– round the blade of the knife and sticks it "into the sheath" (p. 243), after which he closes his eyes in rapture. Lise's encounter with the sheep thief corresponds to Philippa's with Don Juan, but in "The Ring" the seduction duet is consummated.

Lise is brought face to face with a brutal murderer, and it is a powerful confrontation as: "She had never in her life been exposed to danger" (p. 241). On the contrary, she has lived in a protective shell of security and peace of mind, but the irony is that *this* is deadly. The sheep thief is the oppressed nature within Lise's world. He might also prove deadly: if she does not respond to him, he will take revenge, which causes "the horror with which he inspired her" (p. 242). But at the same time: "She was fearless by nature" (p. 242) – and this applies to the risk and insecurity that are natural if one breaks out and creates one's own life, where the sheep thief, as representative of her endeavour, is highly conducive for Lise. Horror is to do with lack of freedom, whilst fearlessness is the prerequisite of freedom. In *Karen Blixen in Denmark: Letters, 1931–62*, Karen Blixen distinguishes between moral strength to overcome fear and genuine fearlessness, about which she says: "Fearlessness is a natural predisposition, which leads a person to thrive in danger, yes, be drawn to it."[100] Lise possesses this genuine fearlessness and is thereby drawn to the sheep thief. In Karen Blixen's work, risk and danger are generally elements of great value; here characters breathe and grow without fear, whereas they shrink and are stifled by horror when they are merely 'safe'. In "The Heroine" Heloise expresses this very precisely: "At moments of risk, it seems one becomes remarkably one's self",[101] and that is exactly what Lise becomes. Her horror shows that she is marked by her upbringing in Grandmamma's milieu, but her fearlessness is evidence that in spite of everything she has preserved the naturalness necessary to encounter the sheep thief. Like Sigismund, she has an understanding that the sheep thief is acting in self-defence, and she knows that he is not an external, but an inner threat, which *she* has the power to fend off.

To sum up, it can be said that the sheep thief and the alcove represent that which is 'dangerous' for the extremely civilised order Lise comes from. In the subversion that occurs, a vital insecurity is generated, encompassing both the risks which promote the individual's progress towards independence and also the inexplicable in life, which prevents stagnation. Meaninglessness, then, has a double meaning: As representative of all that is inexplicable, and blood-covered reality in the form of offence, suffering and death. In sexuality mortal flesh has, however, a perpetual regenerator, which demands its natural right and takes revenge if it does not get it. It demands courage and resolve to recover these forces, lying latent in the alcove and the sheep thief, to consciousness, but Lise has both courage and resolve, and thereby the way is clear for her freedom. The pressing necessity of liberation is apparent from the following passage, which incisively sums up the destructive aspect of Grandmamma's world and at the same time emphasises Lise's faculty of cognition: "After a while she realized that he was observing her just as she was observing him. He was no longer just run to earth and crouching for a spring, but he was wondering, trying to know. At that she seemed to see herself with the eyes of the wild animal at bay in his dark hiding-place: her silently approaching white figure, which might mean death" (p. 241). The specific meaning of death is, of course, that the sheep thief sees a representative of those who want to see him – the murderer – dispatched. Neither can there be any doubt about the symbolism: the white world 'kills' or demonises what the sheep thief represents. The white world *is* death, understood as a world without life – this is where that which is natural in the human perishes, and there is no fertile soil for self-fulfilment.

It is therefore of profound import that Lise saves her life by taking off her wedding ring and offering it to the sheep thief, who kicks it away. Keeping the ring on would have led to certain death, because by so doing she would have persisted in marriage as prescribed by Grandmamma. In removing her wedding ring, and in so doing dropping her handkerchief – her virtue – on the ground, she demonstrates her compliance to the sheep thief, but there is still an ambiguity in her response: "She commanded him, she besought him to vanish as he had come, to take a dreadful figure out of her life, so that it should never have been there. In the dumb movement her young form had the grave authoritativeness of a priestess conjuring down some monstrous being by a sacred sign" (p. 242). In this there lies a final attempt at repression from Lise's side: to continue to be able to follow Grandmamma's rules and keep what the sheep thief – the vampire – represents down in the darkness. But at the same time it is a desire to purge the repression: to remove the tangible "dreadful figure"; and this desire is the strongest – when the sheep thief immediately afterwards kicks away the ring, Lise feels that "things were changed" (p. 242). Thereafter the pairing of Lise and the sheep thief is expressed by the cambric being wrapped around the blade of the knife, and it is made quite clear that it was this that Lise really desired with her behest: "The movement was definitive and unconditional. In this one motion he did what she had begged him to do: he vanished and was gone. She was free" (p. 243). Lise is released in that she recovers for her world that which the sheep thief represents – it is made natural, by means of which the demonic disappears. The sheep thief ceases to exist in the demonic form he had in the state of oppression. The sheep thief "changes the world to the human who faces it" (p. 241), and when Lise has left him she thinks: "All is over" (243), wherewith she is fully aware that the encounter in the forest has disposed of Grandmamma's excessively white world.

Lise is transformed, and this means that the sheep thief is also transformed; in their union "his face under the dirt and sun-tan slowly grew whiter till it was almost phosphorescent" (p. 243). The 'dark' has been excluded from Lise's world and the 'white' from the sheep thief's, but now the light and dark, white and black, pure and impure merge into one another. Lise's trust and warmth remove the demonic from the isolated and tormented sheep thief, and in so doing the extreme in both their situations is brought to an end. In a wider perspective, it is the typical union found in Karen Blixen's work – mind and body, eternity and time, life and death, joy and suffering, meaning and meaninglessness, explanation and inexplicability. This broad and liberating unity of existence, with which both Lise and the sheep thief come in contact, undoubtedly lies behind the use of: "what therefore God has joined together let man not put asunder" (p. 244). Freedom is to be found in acquiescing to the inherent totality, however contradictory that might be. As we have seen, those gods who encompass both sides of life always had Karen Blixen's approval – the Greek, but it could also be the *Old Testament* – for she often refers to the *Book of Job* and thereby to the collaboration between God and Satan. Similarly, she found the natural synthesis preserved in the indigenous peoples of Africa, and in the following passage from *Out of Africa* this implies an ease and freedom:

> *"This assurance, this art of swimming, they had, I thought, because they had preserved a knowledge that was lost to us by our first parents; Africa, amongst the continents, will teach it to you: that God and the Devil are one, the majesty coeternal, not two uncreated but one uncreated, and the Natives neither confounded the persons nor divided the substance."* [102]

"What therefore God has joined together let man not put asunder" (p. 244) is a reference to the traditional marriage ceremony, from which the sentence is an almost exact quotation,[103] but in "The Ring" the sentence fundamentally underlines the inherent totality, which is sabotaged and ruptured in the traditional marriage – the form of marriage that Lise has been brought up to expect, but which she now turns away from. 'Marriage' takes on a different character for Lise, similar to the marriage symbolism used by Søren Kierkegaard in *Either/Or:* "marriage is precisely . . . that infinity which contains finitude, that eternity which contains temporality."[104] Another expression for this union is, in Søren Kierkegaard's writings, the synthesis of soul and body, which is sustained by the spirit, and this is synonymous with the freedom implicit in being *oneself.* One is oneself – with another variation from Søren Kierkegaard for union – when one is in concord with "the universally human" and at the same time cultivates "the particular", by means of which one is different from others. In "The Ring" Lise realises that the destiny she shares with others, the universally human, is far more expansive than she has been brought up to believe – it is the synthesis between light and dark – but she also acknowledges the necessity of acting on one's own initiative, to discharge one's personal destiny. And in discovering the other side of life, her leeway for individual fulfilment is considerably increased.

Immediately after Lise has left the sheep thief, Sigismund catches her up, and calls out a cheerful greeting – even though he must have an inkling of where she has been, as she has not reached further along her route home. Sigismund shows that he is alive to the uncivilised stillness in which Lise has been instructed as "he noticed her silence" (p. 243), and it is made clear that he observes a change in Lise and thereby a change in their relationship: "It was . . . not quite the same hand as he had last kissed" (p. 244). But Sigismund does not attach significance to the lost wedding ring; when Lise tells him that she has lost her ring, he responds: "What ring?" (p. 243), even though it was earlier made clear that the ring was the only piece of jewellery Lise had been wearing.[105] To Sigismund it is merely a ring that can be replaced by another and better one; he is in no way disturbed by the loss of the ring, for he does not attach any value to what it represents: marriage in Grandmamma's sense. Were he, as Leif Søndergaard maintains, a traditional husband and a new father figure, he would have reacted to the loss of the ring with anger, but instead he demonstrates to Lise his role as accomplice in the event. The sheep thief has revealed the masculinity which Sigismund wants to realise in his relationship to Lise; if before she only had one impression of her husband, she is now – in Robert Langbaum's words – "married to two men".[106] The doubleness in the totality can now play its role in their marriage – also because the change that takes place in the sheep thief corresponds to Sigismund's transformation, by means of which Lise and Sigismund can be united. The loss of the ring as an indication of divorce is disclaimed by a forceful emphasis on union at all levels. At the end, Lise's newly-gained awareness and her upholding of a 'self' are asserted: "As she heard her own voice pronounce the words she conceived their meaning" (p. 244). Lise's reply to Sigismund's question about where she may have lost the ring – "I have no idea at all" (p. 244) – is therefore not a lie, but a fully conscious acknowledgement of the 'hidden' and 'secret' as necessary in a realistic marriage.

Lea and Lise

It is very likely that Karen Blixen used a story she had written when young, "The Ploughman"(1907), as the source for "The Ring", which is a more sophisticated version of the earlier story. In "The Ploughman" the forest is an overall representation of everything that is repressed in the light of day – the secret, impenetrable and boundless – and in a wider sense it is a symbol of the untamed aspect and the freedom that disappeared with the onset of civilisation. The forest is the eternity untouched by humans, and therefore the "song of silence"[107] can be heard there, but it is also the domicile of that loneliness which civilisation can remedy. In "The Ploughman", Anders, one of the wild animals of the forest, meets Lea, who conversely is called one of civilisation's tame dogs. She is a young girl in the process of maturing to adulthood. Anders is, moreover, son of a witch, and he is also a murderer, whereas Lea has lived in a strictly controlled environment with – or so she thought – unshakeable values, which have made independent thought redundant. The encounter, naturally, takes place at nightfall while her father is away from home. Lea has been delayed on her way home because her coachman has neglected his duties, about which she is most indignant. The reins have worked loose. Anders explains the murders, of which he has committed many, quite straightforwardly as being the result of the felling of forests, building of roads and making of laws. He is taking revenge on the violation of his territory – a consequence of the process of civilisation. Lea is changed by her encounter with Anders. Her secure world disintegrates, but she is resurrected as an independent agent, in that she draws him into her world. She sets him to work ploughing her field, which speaks for itself and leaves no doubt about his fertile influence on her. But this is also an image of the change that Anders undergoes. His personal force of nature is harnessed to the plough, and he is able to declare that "all is over".[108] He feels liberated as he is no longer ostracised by the civilised world, but now works *in* it. Thus "The Ploughman" ends with the fruitful union of nature and civilisation invalidating the extreme status of both Lea and Anders.

PART III

Life and Tale

Incentive and Repression

Familial influence

In Karen Blixen's childhood home there was a curious mixture of incentive to creativity and intellectual activity, and yet impediment to this if ability wanted to be given free scope. Great inspiration was to be gleaned from her father's writing activities and from having brothers and sisters with broad artistic aptitudes, added to which the education that Karen Blixen received at home was of a very high calibre. On the other hand, there was no expectation of or encouragement to pursue an independent career in the arts – for which Karen Blixen fervently wished – and it was not anticipated that the girls would go into further education. The expectation was that the protection provided by a home education would continue in marriage, and should no marriage take place then the other possibility was to live as an unmarried person in continued dependence on the family. In either eventuality, the scholarship and heightened artistic sense that had been acquired in the childhood home could continue to be safely exercised within the family setting.

The mixed experience in her childhood home was also communicated in the understanding she met from her father and his family and lack of support from her mother's side of the family. Karen Blixen felt that she was in direct and uncomplicated concord with her father's family, whereas her relationship with her mother's family was a constant thorn in her flesh and soul. After the death of her father, when Karen Blixen was only 10 years old, it became difficult to maintain a lifeline to his side of the family – regarded by her mother to be a dangerous influence. Pressure from her mother's family grew, reinforcing Karen Blixen's perception of her father and his family as representative of the positive things in life that were excluded from the upbringing and outlook to which her mother's family subjected her. Throughout her life Karen Blixen saw her father's and her mother's respective families as two opposing attitudes to and implementations of life.

A concise and precise description of what the different families represented is found in Judith Thurman's biography of Karen Blixen. The maternal family was "exemplary bourgeois" and thoroughly middle class. They were traders who had become wealthy through their own ingenuity and frugality and by virtue of the view that life is immoral unless spent in tireless pursuit of a calling. They saw themselves as 'debtors' in relation to existence and were forever engaged in paying off their debt. They were vigorous, but not vital, and there was a touchiness about them as a result of the moral loftiness in which they were unyielding in their demand for humility and in their contempt and fear of the erotic. Piety and the taboos with which they furnished life were also a reflection of their adherence to the Unitarian Church.

Karen Blixen's paternal family, on the other hand, was of an aristocratic disposition, an outer expression of this being their country estate, military officers' lives and kinship with the nobility. They were not concerned about leaving a 'mark', but considered existence to be 'inherited' and a territory in which they had free scope with no moral restrictions. They were virile and spontaneous people, abandoning themselves to the dangerous sides of life, and by so doing found a joy in being alive. For them life was bountiful, and therefore they were also generous. Judith Thurman magnifies the two sides of Karen Blixen's family background as a reflection of a conflict that characterised the general cultural and political atmosphere, and she emphasises that Karen Blixen herself saw her personal background reflected in general contemporary patterns:

> "But if you stand back . . . it is possible to see the two sides as Dinesen herself did, against the background of a great cultural conflict – and then they are face to face. This is the conflict that had emerged in the nineteenth century with the rise of the bourgeoisie, and which Kierkegaard reflected upon in Either/Or (1843), opposing the "ethical" to the "sensuous-esthetic", the instinctual to the moral life. It was this dialectic, much elaborated, that would dominate Danish culture for the rest of the century, and which Isak Dinesen encountered in the literature and philosophy she read as a young woman, in the plays and lectures she attended, in the public debates on sexual freedom and women's rights, and in the political struggles between the conservative aristocracy and the liberal middle class (and later the rising socialist coalition of small farmers and urban laborers)."[1]

There is no doubt that Karen Blixen made use of the personal, for she saw it as an expression of the general, and in so doing she fulfils one of the Danish author and philosopher Villy Sørensen's essential prerequisites: "The prerequisite for an artist to be able to create valid works must be that his inner truth is in accord with the outer reality, so that he cannot avoid but to articulate the problems of his times when he voices his own."[2] But, nevertheless, Judith Thurman goes too far when she rounds off her description by elevating the family poles to a pattern of destiny in which Karen Blixen's ordeals and losses are inevitable. It is quite obvious from Karen Blixen's letters that the prevailing mode of upbringing in the home was a pattern that could have been different – and thus not an upbringing which exempts responsibility.

At a distance from Denmark, in her letters from Africa, Karen Blixen is able to give a clear account of the problems she experienced at home. Rebellion against her home background is present from the start of her stay in Africa, but intensifies as problems with the farm increase and the prospect of returning to Denmark looms relentlessly.

In a letter to her mother, Karen Blixen quite straightforwardly summarises the different familial influences, giving weight to the difference between being oneself and not being allowed to be oneself:

> "I think my greatest misfortune was Father's death. Father understood me as I was, although I was so young, and loved me for myself. It would have been better, too, if I had spent more time with his family; I felt more free and at ease with them. I feel that Mama and Aunt Bess and the whole of your family ... if they care for me at all, do so in a way in spite of my being as I am. They are always trying to change me into something quite different; they do not like the parts of me that I believe to be good." [3]

The families are elevated in a way to powers working for and against freedom, but for Karen Blixen it had been a question of a conscious struggle on the part of her father and mother for what they considered to be in their daughter's best interests. Of her father's suicide she says: "It is really he who is responsible, for he deserted me and must have seen that things were not going to be easy for me." [4] In a letter to her sister, Ellen Dahl, she emphasises that their mother could also be held responsible for having held onto her daughter: "I am thinking of myself in connection with Father's family; I think it would have cut mother to the heart to have had to leave me in their charge, – if she herself could not have kept me, – and yet I believe that I would have thrived on their care ... " [5] In a radio interview with the Danish writer and journalist Karl Bjarnhof [6] Karen Blixen speaks about how her father, who was a conservative aristocrat and captain in the French army during the Franco–Prussian war of 1870–1, felt that his sympathies were at the same time with the Communards; he wrote the book *Paris under Communen* (*Paris During the Commune*) and, moreover, he thereafter settled in primitive conditions among the native Indians of North America. In just such the same way, Babette thrived among both aristocrats and Communards, but does not thrive in the stronghold of morality in Berlevaag. Karen Blixen can

Karen Blixen, 1913
Photograph: Sophus Juncker-Jensen

similarly declare herself on an equal footing with high and low, whereas she considers the middle class to be where the devil, as a manifestation of oppression, has his domain:

> *"if I cannot be with the aristocracy or the intelligentsia I must go down among the proletariat or, what corresponds to that out here, the natives, because I cannot live with the middle class. – The real aristocrats, where they exist, or the proletariat, have nothing to risk. But the middle class always has something to risk, and the Devil is there among them in his very worst, that is to say, his very pettiest form. . . ."* [7]

To Karen Blixen, the aristocratic was a disposition or a lifestyle cutting across class divisions. Just as her father found with the Communards and the North American Indians, she found the aristocratic with the indigenous peoples of Africa – a parallel she was fond of highlighting. As indicated, Babette is born of this ability to thrive with both high and low, but she has also been created to demonstrate the impossibility of living in a middle-class milieu. Babette, however, never liberated herself physically from Berlevaag, but conducted her rebellion in her art, which reflects Karen Blixen's own situation as the artist who, in her work, confronts a milieu from which she personally had difficulties in liberating herself.

When Karen Blixen was 19 years old, she sent Georg Brandes, who at the time was ill, an encouraging greeting in the form of flowers and a letter. Her approach also contained the hope of making contact with the man who "revealed literature to me"[8] and who "might have made a writer or artist of me . . . "[9] But when Brandes later appeared in person at Rungstedlund in order to thank Karen Blixen, her mother sent him away saying that her daughter was not at home. Her mother was using a white lie in order to protect Karen Blixen – who was then fetched from her room to be lectured about her deception, which was how the family viewed her approach to Brandes. The family was indignant that Karen Blixen had done something without their knowledge, and *their* opinion of Brandes was qualified by his reputation as a Don Juan. To Karen Blixen the episode represented her problems at home in a nutshell: overprotection hindering personal development and keeping the spiritual at bay – the lethal effect of anxiety over running a risk, in this instance a sexual risk, but which to Karen Blixen had undoubtedly been an expression of all the beneficial dangers in life for which her family had no appreciation. Karen Blixen had possibly also seen a symbolism in the fact

that Georg Brandes was her father's friend[10] and as a representative of
his world was unable to get a foot through the door of the well-groomed
life at Rungstedlund. The episode demonstrated the consequences of a
pattern of upbringing of which Karen Blixen gives the following description:

> *"if, for instance, from the outset one maintains and educates the race to*
> *believe that it is utterly frightful to let one single hair of a woman's head*
> *be disordered, there will naturally be plenty to do for the rest of her life*
> *running about with parasols or shields of every kind; but in my opinion it*
> *would really be more chivalrous to latch on to the hair a little less, and*
> *neither am I at all certain that the most perfectly set hair in itself is really*
> *more beautiful than freely flowing locks . . . also I myself would prefer*
> *Diana's life to that of Venus, however many rose gardens and dove-drawn*
> *coaches she might have . . . "*[11]

This brings our thoughts back to "The Ring", in which Lise's hair is the
first thing to come under attack when she steps outside her sheltered
world. Of the fortifications in her own childhood home, Karen Blixen is
more ironic and direct: "I think it is possible to live at home and be very
happy there if one can, like the Merman with Agnete, 'stop one's mouth
and one's ears' against the whole of the outside world. I think that is what
all of them at home do . . . "[12] She can, however, also reproach herself for
not – like Lise – early on and resolutely breaking free, but here the explanation or excuse is the incapacitating power of her upbringing at home:
"Of course I should have decided for myself; but here again I met with
that strange opposition to everything that was in any way outside the
narrow circle of home, and that peculiar power they had of always
making one feel in the wrong when one stood out against them."[13]

Karen Blixen often stresses that her family with their goodness and
kindness were not consciously set on doing her harm, but that they acted
blindly in accordance with a pattern of upbringing and an approach to
life which were deep-rooted and indubitable in contemporary bourgeois
Denmark. Nevertheless, this "great unlimited goodness and love"[14] had
a harmful effect because in its one-sidedness and high moral intent it
kept the individual in a position of dependence. This had a paralysing
effect on the emotional life and thinking that ought to form the individual as a free agent; the conflict with parental authority which is vital
to a young person was ruled out: "They made it impossible for me to
show any opposition. You remember we have talked about the strange
power that . . . mother [had] over us . . . to render any criticism, any

contradiction, impossible, to make impossible even one's private thoughts that mother might ever make a mistake, so that it might have been better to dispute with her; this particular capacity has been a fatal influence in my life."[15]

In many of her letters, Karen Blixen describes her endeavours to hold on firmly to the feeling that there actually is nothing to be afraid of in this world, but just endless numbers of "possibilities for beauty".[16] This indicates an inner struggle to overcome an anxiety that emerged from the goodness her family had in telling her how much badness was to be found in the world: "One was surrounded by dangers of the blackest and most extensive kinds: of becoming worldly and vain, of hurting Madame Jensen's feelings, of getting into debt, of not thinking of others, etc. – not to mention the quite dreadful dangers and horrors inherent in everything that had to do with sexual relationships."[17] Where life could have been free and easy, it was made difficult and, against the background of the more natural life in Africa, Karen Blixen writes "absolutely frankly and truthfully"[18] about her childhood and youth in Denmark. Despite appreciation of the best intentions in the family life which she was offered, her conclusion is uncompromising: "all my abilities were destroyed by it; any possibility for me to live and act, achieve something *as myself* came to nothing because of it."[19]

Karen Blixen's overall characterisation of Rungstedlund is "Paradise", and she expresses the wish of being like Lucifer, who rises in revolt and hurtles down from heaven to earth. She clarifies what she means by the symbolic expression "Lucifer":

> "*I conceive of it as meaning: truth, or the search for truth, striving toward the light, a critical attitude, – indeed, what one means by spirit. The opposite of settling down believing that what one cares for is and must be best, indeed, settling into the studied calm, satisfaction and uncritical atmosphere of the Paradise. And in addition to this: work ... a sense of humor which is afraid of nothing, but has the courage of its convictions to make fun of everything, and life, new light, variety.*" [20]

She lists what she ought to have done in her youth to make a break with that Paradise: enjoyed herself at school parties, taken the matriculation examination, married in Paris – or, quite simply, have run away. Particularly painful is her acknowledgement that an early rebellion could have released the artist in her: "I cannot *possibly* write anything of the slightest interest without breaking away from the Paradise and hurtling down to my own kingdom."[21]

Light and Darkness

in Africa

Karen Blixen made herself a new life rich in variety in Africa. Her life there and the country and people she met turned her into "the child of Lucifer".[22] When she became engaged to Bror Blixen, it was their firm intention to settle far away from Denmark, and the departure for Africa was thus an intentional break with her childhood and adolescent environment. In the 'dark continent' of Africa she found a welcome contrast to the white world from which she came. Here was the untamed and spontaneous open-handedness to life she had longed for:

> *"Of course it is rather tiresome that in present-day society adventures almost always mean 'adventures of the heart', when far from everyone has the inclination for that kind of experience; in our way of life that sort of adventure has gradually come to be about the only one people have the chance of getting. But I think that most people have an unconscious feeling that there is more nourishment for soul and spirit in danger and wild hopes, and in this: in hazarding everything, than in a calm and secure existence, and that they are extremely undernourished in this respect, and would give almost everything to the one who can get them this nourishment.*
>
> *This love of adventure and experience is particularly in evidence in my Somalis; every member of that race is happy, whatever happens as long as something is happening; the thing that makes them quite desperate is an uneventful life, – actually, the same can be said about almost all natives."*[23]

It was this kind of aristocratic adventurousness that bound her to her father, and the passage can be taken for a recipe for Babette who invests all her nourishment in an uneventful environment.

Despite constant difficulties in the running of the farm, the work and the environment gave Karen Blixen joy because it was her first independent undertaking. She felt that it grew organically around her, and this was not least due to her relationship with the people who worked on the farm, the indigenous people. She also enjoyed uninhibited association with individuals among the white population, especially the upper-class Englishman Denys Finch Hatton, but in true aristocratic mode an individual could not measure up to a whole people: "it is clear to me by now that my black brother here in Africa has become the great passion of my life, and that this cannot be changed. Even Denys, although he makes me tremendously happy, <u>carries no weight</u> in comparison."[24] It was particularly her independence in daily life and her encounter with the African peoples' fertile imagination and straightforward relationship with the nature within and around them that provided nourishment and prompted Karen Blixen to declare: "here I can be true, I can be myself."[25] In *Out of Africa* she describes how a whole new world opened up for her in Africa, but what was fruitful was not least that it also revealed hidden aspects of herself; as in "The Ring", the image of entering a forest is used:

> *"As for me, from my first weeks in Africa, I had felt a great affection for the Natives. It was a strong feeling that embraced all ages and both sexes. The discovery of the dark races was to me a magnificent enlargement of all my world. If a person with an inborn sympathy for animals had grown up in a milieu where there were no animals, and had come into contact with animals late in life; or if a person with an instinctive taste for woods and forest had entered a forest for the first time at the age of twenty; or if someone with an ear for music had happened to hear music for the first time when he was already grown up; their cases might have been similar to mine. After I had met with the Natives, I set out the routine of my daily life to the orchestra."* [26]

In Joseph Conrad's novel *Heart of Darkness* (1902), Marlow is on a similar journey, leading into the heart of Africa. It is a journey from civilisation back to nature and from history to the unhistorical, but at the same time the actual journey is symbolic of an inner process of awareness – confronting Marlow with his innermost darkness. The novel encompasses a critique of Westerners' conduct in undeveloped countries, but the critique only applies to the abuse – imperialist exploitation – whereas the actual work of spreading so-called civilised conditions is approved, provided altruism and beneficence are the basis of the enterprise. In Karen Blixen's writing, the original African way of life constantly stands out as being superior to the West European – and it should preferably be left untouched.

Heart of Darkness employs a complex nature-symbolism, which, in the first place, identifies the indigenous peoples and the natural environment of which they are a part as a positive counter-picture to civilisation. In this counter-picture, nature is attributed qualities such as freedom, consequence and straightforward self-expression as seen, for example, in the following passage: "The voice of the surf now and then

Karen Blixen in Africa, 1929

was a positive pleasure, like the speech of a brother. It was something natural, that had its reason, that had a meaning. Now and then a boat from the shore gave one a momentary contact with reality. It was paddled by black fellows . . . they had bone, muscle, a wild vitality, an intense energy of movement, that was as natural and true as the surf along their coast."[27] Karen Blixen attributes the same qualities to the indigenous peoples, but to her they are real, they have validity *in* the world, whereas the counter-picture in *Heart of Darkness* ultimately serves to show not merely what is beyond the bounds of civilisation, but that which is eternally absent from the world as such.

The second function of nature-symbolism in *Heart of Darkness* is to demonstrate the oppression of nature that occurs *within* civilisation – of which the outrages committed by colonial powers against natural resources is an extreme illustration. But it is particularly in the portrait of Kurtz's madness that we see the consequences of this oppression of nature. He is the leader of "the Inner Station" – the objective of Marlow's journey – and the demonisation of Kurtz is nature's revenge for his brutal treatment of it. The description of Kurtz's fiancée highlights the fact that oppression is to be found at the very heart of civilisation – this being the London where Marlow visits her when he returns home. She is a Madonna, pure and innocent, but there is also an ambiguity about her: "This fair hair, this pale visage, this pure brow, seemed surrounded by an ashy halo from which the dark eyes looked out at me."[28] Angelic on the surface, but the eyes – which disclose the depths – are dark, and the wording "looked out" implies confinement of the wildness or passion symbolised by the darkness. Karen Blixen uses exactly the same colour symbolism: the dark Babette – compared with an African chief – confined in the Dean's daughters' paradise. Like Conrad, Karen Blixen uses experience from beyond the civilised world, in dark Africa, to illustrate oppression of nature in the white world.

In *Heart of Darkness* nature-symbolism has a third function. The nature that Marlow encounters is also wild and uncontainable, rough and barbaric, and a symbol of eternal emptiness and meaninglessness. As such it is a frightening spectre of the forces that are released if civilisation is removed. This is the fundamental reason for Marlow's return to civilisation, which is thereby acknowledged as a necessary safeguard, a protective illusion, against the awful 'innermost' truths. Karen Blixen did not ignore the roughness and ruthlessness of nature, but it was always also an expression of great beauty – meaning and meaninglessness could not be segregated, and it is generally the harmony which she highlights in the indigenous peoples: "For me the natives always have something deeply poetical about them, like nature itself".[29] Karen Blixen found nothing in Africa that could lead her to excuse anything in the civilisation from which she came.

Her encounter with Africa also occasioned an inner voyage of discovery, along which she found her true self; the inner voyage of discovery in *Heart of Darkness*, on the other hand, results in an acknowledgement that deep down people are "altogether without a substance."[30] That which is indeterminate and indefinable characterises the human and is the fundamental condition of the surrounding environment. In *Heart of Darkness*, however, it has a positive offshoot in the creative power thereby generated: the artist becomes master in his own house, which is the inscrutable ways of reality, the external as well as the inner jungle. Similarly, her encounter with Africa released the creative power in Karen Blixen, and even though she constantly maintains that the one side of existence is profound meaning – the divine – the other side to her view of existence – the demonical uninterpretable and meaninglessness – has many similarities with the insubstantial territory cultivated in Joseph Conrad's universe.

That which the civilised world oppressed in Africa was to Karen Blixen identical with the price to be paid *within* civilisation. The qualities she attributed to dark Africa were of the same character as those squandered in white Europe, and the interplay between light and dark is also acted out in her tales, in which we witness the price of being brought up behind white walls.

In *Shadows on the Grass* she uses hospitalisation in Africa as an image of how the white man pulls up the black peoples' roots. In hospital, the pain, death and uncertainty that were natural elements in the Africans' lives, were hidden – they were admitted to hospital in order to die of boredom instead: "We had been transforming, to them, Rite into Routine. What by now most of all they feared from our hands was boredom, and on being taken into hospital they may well have felt that they were in good earnest being taken in to die from boredom."[31] This takes us back to Søren Kierkegaard for whom "boredom is the root of evil"[32] and a characteristic of the demonised individual who, moreover, he saw in his own time populate Denmark to such an extent that he feared "Old Denmark is foundering – it is a matter of life and death; it is foundering on boredom".[33] According to Karen Blixen, the conduct of the Europeans in Africa stemmed from a total lack of understanding and a blinkered faith in their own infallibility. The price of implementing a process of civilisation must be to blind the dark eyes and replace them with white ones:

> *"We Nations of Europe ... are here turning the blazing lights of our civilization into dark eyes ... We may, if we choose to, I thought further, look forward to the day when we shall have convinced them that it be a meritorious and happy undertaking to floodlight a whole continent. But for that they will have to get other eyes."* [34]

In Karen Blixen's story "The Blue Eyes", the eyes in question belong to a ship's figurehead and are made of precious stones given to the skipper by an African King. When the skipper's wife removes the eyes and replaces them with blue glass from a glazier in Elsinore, the price paid is her blindness and her husband's death. [35]

In 1931 Karen Blixen was forced to give up the farm in Africa, and she looked around frantically for a new opportunity for an independent life so that she could avoid returning to Rungstedlund. She considered herself to be completely happy in Africa, because there she had acquired the essential breadth of outlook and the true freedom from prejudice that enables one to see the infinite richness of life. To leave Africa would be to lose her sight: "To me it would seem the most *natural* thing to disappear with my world here, for it seems to me to be, to quite the same extent as my eyes, or as some talent or other I might have, vital parts of myself". [36] The years spent in Africa had magnified the conflict of interests in relation to her childhood home. To the people who endeavoured to get her to go back there – also for her mother's sake – she responded by saying that she no longer took into account concepts of "sin" and "remorse". It would be "completely and utterly unnatural" to return home: "At home I lose that capacity for taking an overall view that it has cost me so much to attain." [37] Africa had such a hold on her that she not only contemplated but actually attempted to perish with that world: [38] "I still feel that death is preferable to a bourgeois existence, and in death I will confess my faith in freedom." [39]

Displacement and Reflection

in Denmark

Considering the loss of freedom she foresaw for herself in Denmark, it seems incomprehensible that Karen Blixen returned to Denmark anyway and made her home with her mother at Rungstedlund, where they lived together until her mother's death in 1939. But in view of her wretched financial situation after losing the farm and her lack of an education which could qualify her for a job, Karen Blixen must have finally decided that she had no other choice. Her dependence continued – she lived the rest of her life at Rungstedlund, which she inherited jointly with her siblings; however, her earnings as an author gradually gave her greater freedom. *Karen Blixen in Denmark: Letters, 1931–62* bears witness to a continual struggle to find the calm and peace of mind in which to write – problems with her family being a symptom of the displacement that Karen Blixen felt generally in Denmark and in large parts of Western civilisation. Karen Blixen's art, like Babette's, came into being against the odds and as a confrontation with the state of affairs by which she felt herself held captive. Her writing career, after the years in Africa, was a survival project and a way in which to fulfil herself for, as it were, the second time; but even in 1949, when success had long been in the bag, Karen Blixen considered life as a writer to be second-rate in relation to the real life in Africa:

> *"I shall always remain in a way an amateur as a writer. Had I been able to keep my farm, I should never have written any books at all. I have not got the ambition to write, but most certainly the ambition to write well if I write at all. My father . . . always said that professional writing was beneath a man . . . it does somehow apply to a woman as well. I have always felt more at ease amongst sportsmen, farmers, sailors or genuine idlers than amongst literary people."* [40]

Karen Blixen in Denmark: Letters, 1931–62 leaves no doubt that Karen Blixen considered Africa to be her real home and she felt like an exile in Denmark. Babette comes to mind when we read: "one must be prepared to 'belong'; in the long run it just doesn't work to 'come in' from the outside, as the one who has lived in Africa . . . " [41] The difficulty in establishing an affiliation to Denmark is highlighted in the following: "my heart lies buried in the Ngong Hills and here I am like some kind of shadow." [42] In her letters Karen Blixen is therefore often occupied with the possibility of settling in Kenya again. But letters she received from acquaintances in Kenya spoke with one voice of the ever more tragic development in the country, which strengthened her impression that the Kenya she had known had perished. This was the actual reason that she never returned, because "I would feel like a ghost." [43] Life as a shadow where she was and the prospect of a ghostly existence where she wanted to be – this is how the situation looked to Karen Blixen. The changes that had occurred in Kenya meant that it was now part of her past; of her present whereabouts she could but conclude: "It *is* true that Europe – perhaps Scandinavia especially, – is a trap!"[44] In "A Country Tale" we saw how Eitel became a shadow and a ghost when *his* roots were cut off.

Karen Blixen felt isolated and almost persecuted in Denmark. From first to last in her letters from 1931 to 1962, she attacks in biting terms the homeland that threatens to "obliterate me".[45] There is no nourishment to be had because "the Danish character is like dough without yeast",[46] and she particularly regrets the lack of a sense of fun and imagination – in this she also saw the reason for the Danes not understanding her. Her overriding feeling, as during the years before she left for Africa, is of not being able to be herself but, on the contrary, of being inhibited in attaining her full scope. Karen Blixen states that "Denmark has taken my courage from me"[47] and adds: "To create takes tremendous courage!"[48] She describes in detail her own experience of this angst, with which many of the characters in her tales struggle, and in the following passage she uses the example of one of her characters who is badly afflicted in this respect to illustrate her own fate: "Denmark has made more effort to make me afraid than the parson's wife ever did to Alkmene. And it has really been successful in scaring me, in striking terror in my blood . . . "[49] Karen Blixen goes the whole way and uses the 'execution' of Alkmene on the North Common and her lifelessness thereafter on the sheep farm as a picture of the life she herself is in the utmost peril of being sucked into: "I long to see you again, also in order to talk about the North Common, which in the meantime has drawn ominously close . . . I can now, it would seem, be said to be ripe for the sheep farm on the moor."[50]

Life in Africa had made her fearless and brave, but leading a superior existence did not cultivate a need to write. Her great literary works came about in Denmark, even though she found the milieu there suffocating. That is not to say that her writings owe their existence to this milieu, as it can be assumed that Karen Blixen the writer would have flourished in a society that both instilled courage and created the need to write. All the same, like a red rag, Denmark galvanised the writer in Karen Blixen. Her writing is to a considerable extent a confrontation with suffocating environments, and the creative process was a breathing space that safeguarded against total paralysis. Writing provided freedom, and in her letters Karen Blixen also expresses pleasure in the boldness and confidence she experienced when she became recognised

Karen Blixen at Rungstedlund, 1943
Photograph: Olaf Kjelstrup

as an author – this recognition coming, however, from America. She also fortified herself through her conviction that there was a deeper drive that made her writing possible: "la grâce de Dieu", which she also called natural gifts, and which could not be taken from her: "And an artist must as a rule, first and foremost revere la grâce de Dieu and presume that strength of mind will serve it."[51]

Karen Blixen regarded some European countries with great affection, particularly Italy and France, but the openness in respect of all aspects of life with which we have seen her attribute France was in contrast to the paring and repression she found in European civilisation as a whole, and which she considered to be so ominous that revenge was imminent: "The deluge will soon be on us all".[52] For Karen Blixen "interplay" is a fundamental force in the creation of values, but Europe was moving in the completely opposite direction: "all our progress today maintains and leads us towards uniformity, which seems to me to be in itself sterile."[53] Based on this criterion, she criticises equalising democracy, but also Nazi Germany. In 1938 she says of Hitler that "he has great ability", but she has no sympathy for Nazism, for the very reason that it is based on one-sidedness: "This new German manifestation is exclusively *emotive*; I have always objected to that which 'worked upon your feelings', I think that the idea, the truth, – is lacking."[54]

The remedy for the delusions of Europe was, in Karen Blixen's opinion, African wisdom, but she also saw hope for the renewal of civil-isation in the American way of life, without however discussing this in any detail – her viewpoint would seem to be coloured by a private enthu-siasm for the country that acknowledged the significance of her works. At the same time, with her usual contempt for dividing lines, in 1961 she attributed Communism with signs of an understanding for African wisdom – she even contemplated making a trip to Russia to see if this opinion was correct.

Karen Blixen not only considered Kenya, but also America as a possible place of permanent residence. But she stayed in Denmark and kept her difficulties there at a distance by travelling – in Italy, France and America she encountered the generosity and understanding that she missed at home. On the other hand, she did not feel comfortable in Great Britain, which bore the mark of an "idiotised milieu" – she was partic-ularly thinking of the middle-class British in Africa who had conducted themselves like "vandals of the first order".[55] Much to her annoyance she could not reach an agreement with the newspaper *Berlingske Tidende* for a trip to Kenya to write articles about the independence movement there, neither did she fulfil an often voiced wish to make a pilgrimage to Mecca.

Karen Blixen in Denmark: Letters, 1931–62 speaks with uncompromising clarity about the serious illness that often interfered with her work and her travel plans. The illness was the result of chronic mercury poisoning she had incurred during treatment for syphilis. For long periods of the last thirty years of her life Karen Blixen suffered such intense pain that she felt she was "in a completely different world, an underworld".[56] Her greatest resentment was in being unable to exercise the compelling creative energy that she felt despite her illness – when she did succeed in implementing it, writing was "superhuman slave work".[57]

Many of the letters Karen Blixen received expressed recognition of her work. It must have been especially gratifying that a British correspondent, the Africa expert Elspeth Huxley, called *Out of Africa* the hitherto best book about Africa and drew special attention to its mythical quality and power as an enduring monument.[58] There was also encouragement from Danish reviewers, one of whom, Klaus Otto Kapel, writing on the occasion of the publication of *Anecdotes of Destiny*, sets Karen Blixen's mind at ease in relation to the negative reviews in Denmark – these were due to the fact that people were afraid of her because "you show us the price we have had to pay and continue to pay for the welfare state . . . at least there is one person who *dares* to keep and present the accounts".[59] There was recognition from official Danish quarters; she was particularly honoured to receive the Hans Christian Andersen Award, and the group involved with the literary review *Heretica* received her with enthusiasm. This latter relationship remained ambivalent, because, among other reasons, she felt that they saw it "as their business to rebuke me morally. That is something I do not like at all!"[60] From Karen Blixen's point of view, however, these instances of recognition were merely brief interludes in the deluge of animosity from readers, reviewers and publishers in Denmark, who obdurately rejected her persistent attempts to be accepted by and influence Danish intellectual life. She acknowledged sadly that "we are not on the same wavelength",[61] but she also reacted furiously: "It might be absurd, but it is quite indisputable, that spiritually speaking I 'feel unwell' when I turn my thoughts to my Danish audience."[62]

The letters are particularly forthright in Karen Blixen's anger at the reviewers who presented her as aloof from the world and without any interest in ordinary people and problems. She considered it a widespread, but incomprehensible prejudice – whereas she claimed a special knowledge of primitive peoples and the practical cultural work in Africa, which she had continued in her books:

> *"it is a misunderstanding when I am time after time accused of escapism, of not being prepared to 'involve myself' or of having lived and continuing to live in an ivory tower ... Could it be that these reviewers ... forget that I set off on a literary course very late in life, and that I, when this happened, had an almost twenty-year 'involvement' in life and death behind me ... I had, before I wrote my first book, given seventeen years of my life ... to a still ongoing battle, which perhaps cannot be called social, but was however of a practical, universally human type, for the Natives' rights in Africa. It often demanded a tremendous undertaking and often resulted in considerably hard work and onerous consequences. I could certainly have had a more 'entertaining' and harmonious existence out there if I had avoided this problem, as other white women out there did ... I would like to know if any of our 'involved' Danish authors, even Andersen Nexø or Erik Knudsen, have anything like an equivalent social contribution to their credit. One cannot, I think, explain my reviewers' or critics' attitude by saying that they have no way of knowing about this. They have, after all, read* Out of Africa. *Is it not a case that they themselves, in their consideration of the book, remain on a purely aesthetic plane, in a kind of critical ivory tower?"*[63]

This sincerity of tone recurs in many solicitous letters to indigenous Africans, and in the committed dialogue of which the letters as a whole are a manifestation. They radiate a desire to debate, and innumerable letters – to people who were worlds apart – conclude with an invitation to continue the discussion at Rungstedlund. Now and then we see a direct implementation of the philosophy that informs her literary works; this also applies to the detailed advice she was happy to give – with great empathy and an acuteness with which she wanted to open people's eyes. Thus in the following passage from a letter to Thorkild Bjørnvig, Karen Blixen uses the idea of being connected with authentic wildness as a guide for the young writer:

> *"Do you remember that I said I prefer wild animals to tame ... because they, in contrast to these, were in a direct relationship to God? ... This is where human dignity lies: in direct relationship to the gods. That is where the lions' and giraffes' dignity lay, in that they were in direct relationship to an, perhaps unknown to me, African deity. That is why it is terrible to put them in zoos and to place ... people between them and their God ... This is what I now wish for you in Paris: that you, whilst freely and easily*

giving and receiving among people, at the same time feel your own being
to be as unified as a giraffe's or an elephant's on the plain, and just as inde-
pendent and inviolable ... I think you have been watched over too much,
just as unhappy, pampered children are watched over too much. The
human gaze can work like a varnish on the one being observed, closing the
pores of the skin to air and light ... so do not write for any person, nor for
Heretica, and not for any movement or any cultural campaign. But write
because you owe the gods a response."[64]

People, pampered by civilisation, have, like tamed animals, a more
restricted compass for fulfilment. They are made dependent by human
considerations and interests. In order to express eternal nature, the artist
has to break out of this cage. Karen Blixen's call for 'dehumanisation' is
also a call for 'disinterested' art.

There is something both very classical and very modern in Karen
Blixen's works, in that they simultaneously build upon the meaningful
and the meaningless, clarity and the uninterpretable. With her classical
clarity, Karen Blixen subscribes steadfastly in a modern age to the direction, totality and objectivity which modern writers so vigorously reject.
But at the same time it is important to underline that Karen Blixen
stands shoulder to shoulder with the modern writers in their challenge
to merely *representational* realism – like them, she stresses the *creative*
role of art: "Yes, what I most expect and wish and hope for from an
author is that he should be a creator, not just an observer who writes
down what he sees, but that he is able to create his own world, be a fount
not a cistern," as she stated in an interview in 1958.[65] For Karen Blixen
and the modern writers, meaninglessness is also freedom to create, and
this freedom is boundless because one is confronted with "a living thing,
new and soaring and beautiful, impalpable, imperishable", as it is
expressed in James Joyce's novel *A Portrait of the Artist as a Young Man*
(1916).[66] Like Joyce, Karen Blixen could also subscribe to the Einsteinian
universe, in saying: "I now think about myself that I have always uncon-
sciously been an Einsteinian; for instance, I have always been convinced
in my heart that time was an illusion."[67] A basic tenet of realism is the
segregation of past, present and future, but this is alien to Karen Blixen:
"I know that the blunt dividing line which people draw between past
and present is all wrong ... "[68] This is also an explanation of why, with
a few exceptions, her tales are set in times past: "I actually think that
much of what has past, lives just as intensely as that which is present."[69]
The incidence of Greek mythology in Karen Blixen's works contributes
to the existence of the eternal in the present – which is also a modern

feature. The modern novel has a distinct suspension of the time perspective; in James Joyce's *Ulysses*, the modern city of Dublin essentially merges with the Ithaca of Antiquity because the primary endeavour is to depict the eternal, universal human lot from the point of view that history merely generates the same circumstances in different guises. In *Ulysses*, Leopold Bloom notes dryly: "Names change: that's all."[70] This simple disposal of the concept of the modern is also behind Karen Blixen's preference for the eternal themes: when time is an illusion, reality is only to be found in the eternal themes. This has also given her a freedom of choice in the eras during which her tales take place – the difference is, after all, only in names and dates – although she was of the opinion that there were certain periods during which the eternal themes were particularly apparent.

Ulysses goes straight to the point in articulating the historical irony: "we have also Roman law".[71] Karen Blixen shares this disillusioned view of history: "There is, everywhere and at any time, a large portion of devilry, – thirst for power, misanthropy, brutal selfishness and brutal stupidity, – on the part of a large portion of mankind."[72] She points out that she is using the notion of the devil in the prevalent sense for ease of understanding, but that she otherwise thinks highly of this 'gentleman'. At other times, however, Karen Blixen might advance completely contrary views of history, which is in keeping with her other purpose: determination of a direction and pursuit of an objective in which there is the potential for the fulfilment of expectations. Shortly after the end of World War II, she is therefore able to exclaim enthusiastically: "Of myself I can say that during these last few months I have had such a peculiar feeling, which I almost do not dare speak of . . . that a great and wonderful time is drawing near . . . something more far-reaching and momentous, a liberation to something great for a somewhat greater part of the universe!"[73]

In her evaluation of the evil she perceives in the world, Karen Blixen distinguishes between more or less shrouded forms – the worst of which are those that have pinned "the name of Christianity to their infamy".[74] According to Karen Blixen, evil occurs wherever a distinction is made between one's own pure case and the delusions of others, for by so doing the concept of heresy is created and this is the deep-rooted evil. Among many elaborations on this theme, and again with the devil used in the prevalent sense, she writes: "It is the belief in the Devil held by 'the others' . . . which in the individual nature calls forth the Devil incarnate, his being and all his deeds."[75] Karen Blixen adds that the fight against the concept of heresy in all its forms will always be a task for the person who serves freedom of speech.

Karen Blixen clearly rejects Christianity: "I have walked at somewhat of a distance from the path of Christian morality . . . I myself am not, and never have been, Christian."[76] She was very well informed about Christianity, but her conclusion was that there was no historical evidence for it, and she could not understand how the impressions of the people of a small Eastern country should have achieved such significance. It was just one among many and various faiths and she herself had "in my own life received the strongest impression of religious faith through Muhammadans".[77] She brushes aside the Christian ethic of loving one's neighbour by noting that one cannot *do* anything for others "unless one *is* something oneself".[78] And the Christian notion of salvation is anathema to her, because help is only available for the person who – like Babette – "is capable of venturing everything".[79] As we have seen, it is fundamentally the segregations of Christianity and segregations and dividing lines all told that Karen Blixen rejects. This is, not surprisingly, a recurrent theme in *Karen Blixen in Denmark: Letters, 1931–62* and in the following passage it is expressed extremely clearly:

> "*I think it is very wise that in outer-space there is no up or down . . . I simply cannot see that there is any dividing line between nature and man . . . I could imagine that I will be like Shelley's Adonais: "He is made one with nature.' You say that nature has no memory, – but I have often wished that I had a memory like a tree, which carries every single grain inscribed in its being. I am, on the whole, not particularly capable of grasping a 'dualism'.*"[80]

Thought and perception in totalities gives a true picture of the world, whereas falsehood occurs with the splitting of the whole into single parts. In order to create unity, people are naturally equipped with the 'concept': "The person who does not comprehend *the concept* stands apart from human nature."[81] It is false to say that a forest is merely a number of trees, for in the concept of 'forest' the trees assemble and account for themselves; a series of historical events and landscapes are given meaning in the concept of 'homeland'; the concepts x and y are far more truthful than the tangible numbers 5 and 7. Like Plato, Karen Blixen is even of the opinion that the concept precedes representations in reality: "I am of the opinion that for a human being the concept is the reality . . . the concept is the human truth and reality, whatever object it might relate to. A thing *is* that which it *means*."[82] She explains this more simply: "the concept of dog was created before individual dogs, – and in general: create a concept, and the dog will be sure to follow."[83] Karen Blixen saw among her contemporaries a movement away from ideas and concepts; she considered this to be dangerous, because an annihilation of concepts was an annihilation of materialisation. It was not just a spiritual matter, but an issue of far-reaching significance: "When the concept of 'love' is annihilated . . . love undergoes an inflation, which would soon be observed throughout society."[84] Through her art Karen Blixen also wanted to help counteract this disintegration of the natural potential for understanding and action in the world; she considered a great work of literature to be so powerful and groundbreaking that it could "be felt far deeper in society than to those who read it."[85]

At the centre of Karen Blixen's stories is the message about the unwavering significance of art and love. Art could sustain concepts and thereby materialisation, and it was imperative to protect love. Karen Blixen's simple wisdom is that one must be perfectly clear what is of personal importance, and then invest everything in that. It never paid to let matters take their course and try to get off cheaply. It would be all right to try out one's abilities in various directions for a while, but sooner or later one was obliged to assemble one's life in a unity – and she had no hesitation in identifying the unifying factor, as here in a letter to a friend: "You have used yourself well, and have most of the excellent ingredients at your disposal. – What brings them together? – What makes a unity out of all of this? And here I can answer you: *love* does."[86]

Conclusion

The parsonage milieu incurs strong criticism in Karen Blixen's writings. There is, however, a broader objective, the full scope of which the Cardinal in "The Deluge at Norderney" indicates in his characterisation of the paradise that is the milieu's trademark: "I wonder if you would be keen to get in there . . . if you were first allowed a peep into the place. It must be the rendezvous of the bourgeoisie."[1] The description of the Dean's home in Berlevaag is also a cautionary conducted tour of the bourgeois way of life at its worst; the world that is laid bare does not fundamentally distinguish itself from the paradise Svidrigailov describes in *Crime and Punishment*: "But why should it necessarily be enormous? Imagine, instead, that it will be one little room, something like a bath-house in the country, black with soot, with spiders in every corner . . . "[2] That is the punishment for being in breach of life through an ascetic, cubby-hole existence. In her stories Karen Blixen analyses self-denial and charts – with no mitigating circumstances – the route of retribution: one is caught in a spider's web. The message is clear: there is a price to pay for procrastination and neglect; Karen Blixen is a meticulous bookkeeper of the costs. Her assignment was not merely to settle accounts with the state of affairs in Denmark, but in Europe as a whole, and she saw the scale of the problem along the same lines as Nietzsche, who similarly conducted a sweeping campaign against the ascetic ideal, about which he says: "There is hardly anything else I could point out that has pressed so destructively upon *health* . . . particularly of Europeans, as this ideal . . . "[3]

Nor does Karen Blixen accord self-sacrifice any honourable intentions; on the contrary, it is exposed as being in reality an expression of self-absorption. Saving up for the eternal life is an egoistic angst for the definitive death. Humble reticence and the notion of salvation are convenient irresponsibility, upon which God himself passes judgement in "Carnival": "I really should not have created you if I had known that you could do nothing but fall back upon me again."[4] Renunciation is rewarded with the 'good' conscience, which results in an eternal anxiety about one's self and nominates sin as its counter-image, by means of which one can feel superior to others. Protective measures – and thereby the key concepts of security and assurance – are dependent on the notion of an enemy. Karen Blixen shows that the Christian and bourgeois milieu bases its existence on this 'guilt', which it so vigorously rejects, and her criticism can again be brought into sharp focus alongside Nietzsche's comment on the Christian church: "Let anyone dare to speak to me of its 'humanitarian' blessings! To *abolish* any distress ran counter to its deepest advantages: it lived on distress, it *created* distress to externalise *itself*. The worm of sin, for example: with this distress the church first enriched mankind."[5] Morality claims eternal significance, but is actually self-contrived and as such a personal and time-bound provision.

On every level, authorities which separate and split up are denounced; they prohibit a nature-given, eternal context and thereby ensure ignorance of fundamental forces in life. Karen Blixen is firm in her attribution of responsibility where these milieux are concerned – they are certainly not let off with reference to preordained destinies. On the contrary, she is very specific in her imputation of how much *in reality* could be different. Destruction as a consequence of splitting up can be held responsible because it is time-bound, which also implies trust, as time-bound authorities are transitory. Accordingly, in the depiction of the institution of marriage and pattern of upbringing, we see enough examples of the individual being split irreparably – but at the same time a number of mutinies are carried through. The works show that there is a fulfilling reality: an abandonment to wild hope, accompanied by action and rebellion.

The pronounced incidence of 'orphans' in the tales is an expression of lack of genuine parental authority. A bleak picture of the relationship between children and adults is painted. It is characterised by absence of contact, due to adults losing touch with their childlike and playful natures, which children therefore have to fight a hard battle to preserve. This battle is also a picture of prevailing conditions for the modern person; adults are representatives of a period that, in its one-sided focus on the material and rational, has eliminated imagination and spontaneity. In other words, the period is based on the masculine and ignores the feminine, contributing to this rootless enterprise. Karen Blixen stated in "Oration at a Bonfire, Fourteen Years Late": "And out of deep personal conviction I wish to add that precisely our small society – in which human beings have achieved so much in what they are able to do and in the concrete results they can show – needs people who are. Indeed, our own time can be said to need a revision of its ambition from *doing* to *being*."[6] Contemporary society moves on the purely human level, but can be changed by making room for the unchangeable; time needs eternity – and Karen Blixen's aristocratic art is a response to this.

The works contain a broad critique of civilisation; the assertion is not, however, that civilisation in itself is restricting, as certain forms of civilisation – France, for example – can embrace freedom. In Karen Blixen's view, the integrated French orientation was in pact with nature, but this pact was perverted in the major part of West European civilisation, whose violation of the natural values in Africa was simply the lamentable exhibition of its own impoverishment. Like the ancient Greeks, the indigenous peoples were true aristocrats, and in the subversion of the original Africa, Karen Blixen undoubtedly saw a repetition of the bourgeois transformation of Europe. Domestication was the measure employed by the bourgeois citizen everywhere. He was trained to "*hold in contempt* all coarse, tempestuous, unbridled, hard, violent-predatory health and powerfulness", as Nietzsche says of the ascetic priest.[7]

To Karen Blixen, Africa represented high culture and wildness simultaneously – with the proviso that innate wildness was the prerequisite of high culture. In the essay "Farah" she states that the Africans were like children or adolescents – this being unconditional praise of their integrated, self-respecting, imaginative and untamed hearts.[8] Farah himself is characterised as the perfect gentleman and also "at heart a wild animal".[9] Karen Blixen was fond of saying that hunters and lions become as one during a lion-hunt; she is not merely highlighting how closely the human and the animal correspond with one another, but in a wider sense giving a picture of the human being's fortunate encounter with the wildness in himself. The lion thus becomes a perfect gentleman; for Karen Blixen this is the image of optimal human freedom and mode of existence: "A lion on the plain . . . is the realisation of human generations' notion of consummate autonomy and indomitability. It was the greatest honour for the great kings to be called Lionheart."[10]

In Karen Blixen's universe, freedom is only found where the forces of nature have scope for expression. Thus, her works insist on giving erotic feeling the room which "one of the greatest and most violent of life's forces"[11] *must* have. Erotic feeling is a supreme manifestation of life and an eternal source of strength – to gain access to which one is perfectly entitled to transgress moral codes. If the erotic is not allowed to take its course, it asserts itself as demonisation, which is the real sin; it intervenes, whether we want it to or not.

Karen Blixen also considers the erotic to be a crucial factor behind decisions that pass themselves off as personal choice. Therefore she is of the opinion that it is not the selection of a particular partner – the individual may on the contrary be chosen quite by chance – but "the force of erotic feeling"[12] as such that leads to love affairs and marriage.

The forces of nature achieve full expression when, in the aristocratic manner, one has the unity of the divine and the demonic in one's backbone. Should one not be fortunate enough to belong to a cultural set or milieu that lives according to this natural twofoldness, one has to acknowledge it and thereby rescind the unnatural schism. This is the message, first and last, in Karen Blixen's writings; in the outline of her works we can see a total exposition of this twofold vision in a poem from her teenager years and in her first published story, "The Hermits", written when she was 22 years old. That this should have been her outlook at such an early age is undoubtedly due to her experiences growing up with her family and her youth spent at Rungstedlund. But we have also seen that this twofold vision received sustenance and inspiration from sources such as *The Old Testament* and Greek mythology, Steen Steensen Blicher, Emil Aarestrup and Sophus Claussen – to say nothing of the profound affirmation she found in the Africans' original world picture. Karen Blixen is part of a long tradition, which can be summed up in the wisdom that many of the characters in the Danish author Henrik Pontoppidan's works achieve. There is Torben Dihmer in the novel *De Dødes Rige* (*The Realm of the Dead*, 1912–16), who, at the end of his life reaches the "conviction that a happier time would come for the world than the one he himself had experienced, a time when human beings with a shudder would turn from the artificial sterilised existence, the daylight hell in which they now floundered in a daze, and again without contradiction take the bad with the good from life's eternal fount and drink in nourishment from the darkness as well as from the light."[13] And in the story "Rejsen gennem Livet" (Journey through Life, 1930) old King Anders, at the end of the journey, feels a childlike joy in nature and a special concord with the skylarks: "Now he was their equal. Past and future melted for him into joyous moments where the boundaries of life and death were eradicated, earth and heaven became one."[14] As with Karen Blixen, this is a case of redemption; Peter Høeg is one of the modern authors to have followed up the tradition after Karen Blixen, but in his works the doubleness appears strangely characterised by the unconsummated and breathless, which is reflected in a more prosaic form of expression: "she saw ... that what the grand scheme of things amounted to was a perpetual act of unconsummated, uninterrupted coitus between heaven and earth. Then she lay down again and went back to sleep" – as we read in *The Woman and the Ape*.[15]

Karen Blixen's works do not take creation as a pretext for

sleepwalking, but as an ocean of inexhaustible opportunities that *demand* to be taken advantage of. She demonstrates an uncommonly embracing *acceptance* of created life. The given setting is accepted without reservation – the only objection is to human mismanagement. Life incorporates assets of such significance that it is worth offering everything for them. Each individual has to identify personal priority and have the courage to stake everything on realising it – the reward is then a completely true life. Conversely, misfortune is having to acknowledge that one has made oneself "too small for the ways of God", as the dying Prince Potenziani, in deep sorrow, recognises in "The Roads Round Pisa".[16] The inexhaustible scope of creation gives the individual limitless opportunity also to be a creator – the conception of the idea alone is proof that there *is* a direction and an objective. The person who wants to take initiative will find much encouragement in Karen Blixen's writings – further reinforced by initiative also being seen as testimony to unlimited resources *within* the individual. Inexhaustibility is correspondingly a part of the human make-up, and it is therefore a restriction to settle on a single fixed identity.

'Aristocrat' is Karen Blixen's hallmark for the person who lives out the eternal order of existence in this way. Such conduct equips the individual with the Greek meaning: the best (*aristo*) power (*kratos*). There is nothing *between* the aristocrat and life, *as it is*, therefore the underlying powers *are* his or her strength. Vitality originates in direct access to the sources: there is no hindrance in the form of a regulating morality. The true aristocrat is totally permeated by the impersonal, and consequently there is no actual individuality to offer up when he dies for these higher assets. There is nothing to lose because, for the aristocrat, eternity is not life after death, but that which always is. Fearlessness is thus an expression of total unfamiliarity with the notion of 'loss' – which does not come into the equation until one sells out of the aristocratic assets, and then honour is no longer intact. Fearlessness is also the mark of the individual unable to live without risk, for that would be the same as cutting oneself off from a section of life. Courage is actually just a question of coming to grips with the adventures life itself offers. If one has a zest for life, there is no end to it – therefore the aristocrat can, without any more ado, happily go forth and be unsparing. The aristocratic perspective is central to Karen Blixen's writings, as the epitome of the *genuine*.

Karen Blixen's tales have themselves as the theme to the extent that they set down the aesthetic from which they are written. Karen Blixen's aristocratic art is sustained by the great ambition to reflect the world *genuinely*, and in this lays the conviction that art can become "God's mouthpiece",[17] with God also comprising the demonic. This presupposes, naturally, that the artist is the aristocrat, completely permeated by the impersonal view he disseminates; thereby he is not just an instrument, but also the creator – by virtue of the demonic boundlessness. The artist must, without prejudice, disseminate all aspects of reality – but this also implies a free interpretation, as it is only by means of this that he can render the aspects open for interpretation. The work of art must have the clarity and irrationality of existence, and thus the artist must both transilluminate and continually entrust to the imagination. Freedom from prejudice is the demand for a completely impersonal perspective on the part of the artist: he must proceed inhumanly, in that personal manifestos, compassion, the desire for reconciliation, etc. must not obstruct the supra-individual context he has to depict. The artist must show the existence that goes beyond the individual sphere, and if he allows himself to be swayed by pity he will paralyse the storyline and the characters who appear in it.

Eternity must lie at the core of the work of art, along with those products of the course of time that have their origin in the eternal; the foundation is secured by an undercurrent of the myths, fairy tales and stories which are composed of the immortal material – the immortal literature is that 'lineage' from which the work of art emerges and that it carries forward. But, on the external plane, the work of art must also deal with constraints of time and place, which are in opposition to the true state on the inner plane. There must be an exposition of the concrete repercussions of constraints, but the contrast will make it quite clear as to what is obstructed by these constraints – what they cannot in the long run restrict. The external plane is destroyed from within, and there is an openness to acknowledgement of what is significant and insignificant in existence. The work of art thus becomes a source of acknowledgement and liberation; in addition, it facilitates direct change, for the formation of other notions of reality is in itself a transformation of that reality. The aristocratic art is thus far from unworldly, but rather a profound involvement; it does not merely galvanise to debate and action, but is in itself an action with direct influence on the state of affairs in society. The prerequisite is, of course, that the work is read: for Karen Blixen the immortal story is just as essential as water.

Notes

INTRODUCTION

1 *Karen Blixen i Danmark: Breve 1931–62*, edited by Frans Lasson and Tom
  Engelbrecht, Gyldendal, Copenhagen, 1996, vol. 2, p. 597. The letters,
  published in two volumes, are not found in an English-language translation.
  Hereafter referred to as *Karen Blixen in Denmark: Letters, 1931–62*. The speech
  was held for the Danish author Tom Kristensen, who received *Boghandlernes
  Gyldne Laurbær* (The Booksellers' Association annual literary award) in 1955.
  Karen Blixen addressed the audience at the award ceremony in Restaurant
  Nimb, Copenhagen, 19 February 1955. Her speech is reproduced in its entirety
  in vol. 2 of the letters, pp. 595–8.

2 Ibid., vol. 2, p. 597.

3 "Peter and Rosa", *Winter's Tales*, Penguin Books, 1983, p. 149.

4 Ibid., p. 170.

PART I   KAREN BLIXEN'S WORKS

1 *Karen Blixens Tegninger* [*Karen Blixen's Drawings* – not currently found in
  an English-language translation], publ. by Forening for Boghaandværk, 1969,
  p. 26. This book consists of two essays – "Til fire Kultegninger" (Of Four
  Charcoal Drawings) and "To Malerier" (Two Paintings) – in which Karen
  Blixen writes about her drawings and paintings and her thoughts on the art
  of painting. The book is illustrated with a selection of Karen Blixen's drawings and paintings. At her home, Rungstedlund, which is today The Karen
  Blixen Museum, there is a gallery exhibiting her drawings and four oil paintings that she painted in Africa.

2 Ibid., p. 32.

3 Ibid., p. 26.

4 Ibid., p. 26.

5 Ibid., p. 26.

6 *The Life and Destiny of Isak Dinesen*, collected and edited by Frans Lasson,
  text by Clara Selborn, Random House, New York 1970 (*Karen Blixen. En
  digterskæbne i billeder*, publ. Gyldendal 1969/1979, p. 42. The poem is not in
  the English-language edition; the Danish edition states that the poem was
  written when Karen Blixen was between 15 and 20 years old.)

7 Ibid., p. 42.

8 *Letters from Africa, 1914–1931*, The University of Chicago Press, 1981 (*Breve fra*

Afrika, 1914–31, edited for The Rungstedlund Foundation by Frans Lasson, Gyldendals Paperbacks 1978/1991), translated by Anne Born, pp. 256–7, letter dated 16/5–1926.

9 *Karen Blixen in Denmark: Letters, 1931– 62*, vol. 2, p. 446, letter dated 4/10–1960.

10 *Letters from Africa, 1914–1931*, p. 256, letter dated 16/5–1926.

11 In *'Isak Dinesen' and Karen Blixen – The Mask and the Reality*, by Donald Hannah, Putnam & Company, London, 1971. Appendix: *The Revenge of Truth: A Marionette Comedy*, translated by Donald Hannah, p. 195.

12 Ibid., pp. 181–2.

13 *Letters from Africa, 1914–1931*, pp. 363–4, letter dated 10/6–1928.

14 *The Revenge of Truth*, p. 186.

15 *Carnival – Entertainments and Posthumous Tales*, Heinemann, London, 1978. (*Karneval og andre fortællinger*, Gyldendal, 1994.)

16 *Osceola*, publ. Gyldendal 1962, p. 70. Not currently found in an English-language translation.

17 Ibid., pp. 87–8.

18 *Karen Blixen in Denmark: Letters, 1931–62*, vol. 1, p. 234, letter dated 8/12–1936, written in English.

19 Ibid., vol. 1, p. 180, letter dated 29/1–1935.

20 In "On Mottoes of My Life", Karen Blixen states that she wrote two of the *Seven Gothic Tales* in Africa (*Daguerreotypes and Other Essays*, translated by P. M. Mitchell and W. D. Paden, Heinemann, 1979, p. 11; *Essays*, Gyldendal, Copenhagen, 1965). In *Karen Blixen in Denmark: Letters, 1931–62* she states: "when I wrote 'The Roads Around Pisa' in Africa" (vol. 1, p. 567, letter dated 14/2–1950) and "when I began writing 'The Monkey' in Africa" (vol. 2, p. 434, letter dated 21/2–1960). Gustav Mohr, in a letter to Karen Blixen dated 16/8–1934 (vol. 1, p. 163), writes that he first read "The Roads Around Pisa" and "The Old Chevalier" "3 or 4 years ago", which would have been in Africa.

21 *Karen Blixen in Denmark: Letters, 1931–62*, vol. 1, p. 140, letter dated 7/6–1934.

22 Ibid., vol. 1, p. 85, letter written during the summer of 1932. The letter, written in English and sent by Thomas Dinesen to the American writer Dorothy C. Fisher in order to ask her opinion about the possibility of publishing *Seven Gothic Tales* in America, was actually drafted by Karen Blixen.

23 Ibid., vol. 1, p. 134, letter dated 5/5–1934. Underlining in the letters indicates words or phrases written in English.

24 *Letters from Africa, 1914–1931*, p. 334, letter dated 13/1–1928.

25 *Seven Gothic Tales*, Penguin Books, 1963, p. 8.

26 *Letters of Fyodor Michailovitch Dostoevsky to his Family and Friends*, translated by Ethel Colburn Mayne, Peter Owen Limited, London, 1962, p. 167.

27 *Seven Gothic Tales*, p. 167.

28 Ibid., p. 167.

29 Ibid., p. 159.

30 Ibid., p. 98.

31 Ibid., p. 112.

32 Ibid., p. 112.
33 *Karen Blixen in Denmark: Letters, 1931–62*, vol. 1, p. 60, letter dated 17/2–1931.
34 Ibid., vol. 2, p. 434, letter dated 21/2–1960.
35 Gramophone recording, *Karen Blixen fortæller* [*Karen Blixen Tells Stories*] (Louisiana LGLP 3002, 1960), on which the tale is called "Kong Herodes' Vin" [King Herodes' Wine]. Also available as audio cassette tape (EXL 40 20047, 1991).
36 *Out of Africa*, Penguin Books, 1954, p. 30.
37 *Seven Gothic Tales*, p. 170.
38 Aage Henriksen, *De ubændige* [*The Indomitable*], Gyldendal, Copenhagen, 1984, p. 87.
39 *Winter's Tales*, Penguin 1983, p. 178.
40 *De ubændige* [*The Indomitable*], pp. 83–8.
41 *Winter's Tales*, p. 175.
42 Ibid., p. 177.
43 Ibid., p. 196.
44 Ibid., pp. 196–8.
45 *Seven Gothic Tales*, pp. 171–2.
46 In "On Mottoes of My Life" Karen Blixen writes: "As I look from the one age to the other, I find this particular idea – the word, *le mot*, and the motto – to be one of the phenomena of life which in the course of time have most decidedly come down in value. To my contemporaries the name *was* the thing or the man; it was even the finest part of a man, and you praised him when you said that he was as good as his word." *Daguerrotypes and Other Essays*, p. 1.
47 *Winter's Tales*, p. 178.
48 Ibid., p. 39.
49 Ibid., p. 49.
50 Odense University Press, translated by Anne Born, 1985, p. 94. (*Dianas Hævn – to spor i Karen Blixens forfatterskab*, Odense Universitetsforlag, 1981.)
51 Ibid., p. 94.
52 Ibid., p. 96.
53 *Winter's Tales*, p. 70.
54 Ibid., p. 75.
55 *Letters from Africa, 1914– 1931*, pp. 336–7, letter dated 13/1–1928.
56 *Karen Blixen in Denmark: Letters, 1931–62*, vol. 1, p. 300, letter dated 15/7–1939. This is how Karen Blixen puts it whilst working on "Alkmene", but there is also direct reference to Shakespeare's *The Winter's Tale* in the story itself.
57 "The Book of Daniel", ch. 5, v. 26.
58 *Karen Blixen in Denmark: Letters, 1931–62*, vol. 2, p. 243, letter dated 18/9–1954.
59 *Winter's Tales*, p. 98.
60 *Seven Gothic Tales*, p. 241.
61 *Karen Blixen in Denmark: Letters, 1931–62*, vol. 1, p. 443, letter dated 24/4–1946.

62 Ibid., vol. 1, p. 382, letter dated 2/11–1944.
63 *Gengældelsens Veje* [*The Angelic Avengers*] Gyldendals Tranebøger 1967, p. 82. This sentence is not found in the English version.
64 *The Angelic Avengers*, Random House, 1947, pp. 158–9.
65 Ibid., p. 263.
66 Fyodor Dostoevsky, *Crime and Punishment*, translated by Jessie Coulson, W. W. Norton & Company, New York, 1964, p. 276.
67 *The Angelic Avengers*, p. 262.
68 Ibid., p. 176.
69 Bodil Ipsen and Ingeborg Brams were leading Danish actresses. Bodil Ipsen's reading of "Babette's Feast" is available on a gramophone recording (Danica DLP 8128) and audio cassette tape (Danica DMC 8128).
70 *Daguerreotypes and Other Essays*, Heinemann, London, p. 2.
71 "The Ghost Horses", in *Carnival – Entertainments and Posthumous Tales*, publ. Heinemann, London 1978, p. 261.
72 Ibid., p. 251.
73 *Karen Blixen in Denmark: Letters, 1931–62*, vol. 2, p. 120, p.160 and p. 270, letters dated 19/12–1952, 25/10–1953 and 1/3–1955.
74 Ibid., vol. 2, p. 329, letter dated 25/9–1956.
75 Ibid., vol. 1, p. 543, letter dated 29/12–1949.
76 Ibid., vol. 2, pp. 160–1, letter dated 25/10–1953.
77 "Second Meeting" is in *Carnival – Entertainments and Posthumous Tales*.
78 *The Odyssey*, translated by A. T. Murray, Harvard University Press, Cambridge, Massachusetts/William Heinemann Ltd, London, 1974, vol. 1, p. 19.
79 Ibid., vol. 1, p. 135.
80 Henrik Ibsen, *The Wild Duck*, translated by Michael Meyer, publ. Methuen & Co Ltd, London , 1968, p. 44.
81 James Joyce, *Ulysses*, Penguin Books/The Bodley Head, 1969/1984, p. 208.
82 *Last Tales*, Penguin Books, 1986, p. 200.
83 *Karen Blixen in Denmark: Letters, 1931–62*, vol. 1, p. 470, letter dated 23/7–1947.
84 Ibid., vol. 2, p. 160 and pp. 328–9, letters dated 25/10–1953 and 25/9–1956.
85 *Ehrengard*, Random House, New York, 1963, p. 35.
86 Ibid., p. 38.
87 *Samlede essays* [*Collected Essays*] is an enlarged edition of *Mit livs mottoer og andre essays* (1978) [*On Mottoes of My Life and Other Essays*], which was itself an enlarged edition of *Essays* ([*Essays*], 1965). Most of the essays are found in *Daguerreotypes and Other Essays*. This is the case with three of the four essays discussed in this section. The fourth essay mentioned, "On Modern Marriage and Other Observations", was published in English as an independent book. (See note 88).
88 *On Modern Marriage and Other Observations*, translated by Anne Born, St. Martin's Press, New York, 1977, p. 74.
89 Ibid., p. 57.

90 Ibid., p. 56.

91 Ibid., p. 36.

92 As Sten Eiler Rasmussen recounts from a conversation he had with H. C. Branner about Karen Blixen's essay. Radio broadcast: *Karen Blixen og fortællingen om Spøgelseshestene* [*Karen Blixen and the tale about The Ghost Horses*], Danmarks Radio, 30/1–1971.

93 *Daguerreotypes and Other Essays*, p. 12.

94 *Karen Blixen in Denmark: Letters, 1931–62*, vol. 1, p. 390, letter dated 16/11–1944.

PART II   WHEN DESTINY COMES CALLING

1 I have previously set out these considerations of Karen Blixen's concept of destiny and the ensuing discussion of her views on art in an article: "Karen Blixens sande historie" [Karen Blixen's True Story], Københavns Folkeuniversitets prospectus, *Sommeren 96*, April 1996.

2 In the journal *Vindrosen* I, no. 5.

3 *Anecdotes of Destiny*, 1958. All quotations from *Anecdotes of Destiny* are taken from the Penguin Books edition, 1986.

4 *Last Tales*, p. 22.

5 *Carnival – Entertainments and Posthumous Tales*, p. 71.

6 *Karen Blixen in Denmark: Letters, 1931–62*, vol. 1, p. 278, letter dated 1/6–1938. There is no indication of which painting by Degas she is referring to, nor when Karen Blixen saw it. She merely states that it had previously hung in the Palais du Luxembourg in Paris and that in 1938 it was hanging in the Louvre.

7 *Carnival – Entertainments and Posthumous Tales*, p. 71.

8 *Fodreise fra Holmens Kanal til Østpynten af Amager* (*Walking Tour from Holmen's Canal to the Eastern Point of Amager*), DSL/Borgen 1986, p. 98.

9 *Last Tales*, p. 100.

10 Ibid., p. 102.

11 *Karen Blixens Tegninger* [*Karen Blixen's Drawings*], p. 23 with the drawing reproduced on p. 25. It is on display in the gallery at The Karen Blixen Museum.

12 *Last Tales*, pp. 23 and 24.

13 *Daguerreotypes and Other Essays*, p. 179.

14 *Last Tales*, p. 21.

15 *Last Tales*, p. 23.

16 Ibid., p. 23.

17 *Seven Gothic Tales*, p. 239.

18 Ibid., p. 142.

19 *Daguerreotypes and Other Essays*, p. 191.

20 In the analysis of "The Ring", the secretive in Karen Blixen's work will be compared with Steen Steensen Blicher's concept of it in *"Sildig Opvaagnen"* [Tardy Awakening].

21 In *Ladies' Home Journal*.

22   *Karen Blixen in Denmark: Letters, 1931–62*, vol. 2, p. 335, letter dated 17/11–1956.

23   This is Karen Blixen's own version in "The Immortal Story" of a passage in *The Book of the Prophet Isaiah*, ch. 35.

24   Judith Thurman, *Isak Dinesen: The Life of Karen Blixen*, Penguin Books, 1984, p. 366.

25   "Babette's Feast" was published in Jørgen Claudi's Danish translation in 1952, but it was Karen Blixen's own Danish version that was later included in *Anecdotes of Destiny*.

26   *Isak Dinesen: The Life of Karen Blixen*, pp. 366–7.

27   For the present analysis, the 1958 version of "Babette's Feast" in the edition of *Anecdotes of Destiny* referred to in note 3 has been used. This is Karen Blixen's own enlarged and improved version of the original story printed in *Ladies' Home Journal* in 1950. But it should be noted that the indications of time in *Anecdotes of Destiny* differ from the dates in the original version. In *Ladies' Home Journal* it is stated that 16 years pass between the first and second episodes and 14 years between the second and last episodes, the tale thus ending in 1885. These same dates are used in Karen Blixen's own Danish version of "Babette's Feast" in the Danish edition of *Anecdotes of Destiny* [*Skæbne-Anekdoter*] from 1958. But in consideration of the overall text, this Danish version is more in agreement with the version from the English-language edition of *Anecdotes of Destiny*. It may seem surprising that Karen Blixen changed the dates from the original version as that is actually the most precise, which is an obvious reason for keeping these dates in the Danish version. In the English-language version in *Anecdotes of Destiny*, the elastic has to be stretched for the first episode to span two years; likewise, there is here uncertainty in the dates stated in the last episode about how long ago it was that Loewenhielm first visited the sisters: it ought to be 29 years, but in some places it says 30 years, other places 31 years. As the tale ends in 1883, we are given both 1853 and 1852 as the date for the beginning of the tale – instead of the correct 1854. But this could be explained away as use of the vague phrase '30–or–so years ago'.

28   *Kierkegaard's Writings, III; Either/Or, I*; edited and translated by Howard V. Hong and Edna H. Hong; Princeton University Press, 1987, pp. 87, 88, 90. In a letter to her brother Thomas Dinesen, Karen Blixen recommends that he read Søren Kierkegaard: "And by the way, read Søren Kierkegaard, too, . . . I know that we have 'Either/Or' at home, anyway. I do not think that anyone can read him closely without being gripped by him." *Letters from Africa, 1914–1931*, pp. 225–6, letter dated 3/8–1924.

29   Søren Kierkegaard, *The Concept of Anxiety*; edited and translated by Reidar Thomte in collaboration with Albert B. Anderson; Princeton University Press, 1980, p. 75.

30   Martin A. Hansen, *The Liar*, translated by John Jepson Egglishaw, Quartet Books, London, 1986, pp. 97–8.

31   *The Gospel According to St. Luke*, chapter 10, verses 38–42.

32 *The Epistle of Paul the Apostle to the Ephesians*, chapter 2, verses 20–2.

33 *The First Epistle General of Peter*, chapter 2, verse 8.

34 *Letters from Africa, 1914–1931*, p. 62, letter dated 27/2–1918.

35 *Shadows on the Grass*, Penguin Books 1984, pp. 22–4.

36 *Letters from Africa, 1914–1931*, p. 61, letter dated 26/2–1918.

37 Ibid., pp. 53–4, letter dated 13/9–1917.

38 *The Book of Psalms*, Psalm 91, verses 10–13.

39 Bengt Holbek and Iørn Piø, *Fabeldyr og sagnfolk* [*Fable Animals and Mythical People*], Politikens Forlag, 1967, pp. 330–1.

40 *Out of Africa*, p. 261.

41 Sophus Claussen, *Djævlerier* [Diableries], Gyldendal, Copenhagen, 1904, pp. 170–1.

42 *Letters from Africa, 1914–1931*, p. 136, from a letter dated 15/10–1922. The Danish title of the poem referred to as "Aphrodite's Vapors" is "Aphrodites Dampe".

43 Ibid., p. 155, from a letter dated 6/5–1923.

44 Karen Blixen does not quote the poem quite correctly.; the second line should read "a boastful flash from his fiery tail of stars" (as pointed out in *Letters from Africa, 1914 –1931*, note 247, p. 440). The letter to Thomas Dinesen referred to: *Letters from Africa, 1914– 1931*, p. 247, from a letter dated 1/4–1926.

45 *Diableries*, p. 23.

46 This is from an English hymn taken from the Latin, *Take Not Thought*, anon.

47 J. Henriksson, *Växterna i de gamlas föreställningar, seder och bruk* [*Plants in the Concept of the Old*], Redviva, Stockholm 1975, p. 33.

48 V. J. Brøndegaard, *Folk og Flora. Dansk Etnobotanik* [*Folk and Flora: Danish Ethnobotany*], Rosenkilde og Bagger, 1978, p. 74.

49 Ibid., p. 75.

50 *The Second Book of Moses*, chapter 22, verse 18.

51 *Daguerreotypes and Other Essays*, p. 33.

52 Ibid., p. 35.

53 Ibid., p. 34.

54 Ibid., p. 35.

55 Ibid., p. 33.

56 Johnny Thiedecke, *De satans kvinder – En heksehistorie* [*Damned Women – A Story of Witches*], Panheon, 1990, p. 50.

57 From the 13th century. The theory is here presented according to Bent Funder and Rasmus Hansen, *Hekse* [*Witches*], Systime, 1985.

58 Ibid., p. 56.

59 Johnny Thiedecke, *De satans kvinder – En heksehistorie* [*Damned Women – A Story of Witches*], p. 46.

60 Bent Funder and Rasmus Hansen, *Hekse*, p. 9.

61 *The Gospel According to St Luke*, chapter 14, verse 11.

62 Ibid., chapter 14, verses 26 and 33.

63 Ibid., chapter 22, verse 27.

64 From Emil Aarestrup's poem "Paa Maskeraden" ["At the Masquerade"], 1826; *Udvalgte digte* [*Selected Poems*], DSL/Borgen, 1998, pp. 165–6.

65 *The Fourth Book of Moses, called Numbers*, chapter 13, verse 23.

66 *The Gospel According to St Mark*, chapter 11, verses 23–4.

67 *Anecdotes of Destiny*, pp. 4–5.

68 In *The Pact – My friendship with Isak Dinesen*, translated by Ingvar Schousboe and William Jay Smith, Louisiana State University Press, Baton Rouge and London, 1983, p. 56 (Thorkild Bjørnvig, *Pagten*, Gyldendal, 1974/1985).

69 Johannes Møllehave, *Lyst, pligt og øllebrød* [*Desire, Duty and Ale-and-bread-soup*], Politiken newspaper, 10/10–1987.

70 *The Book of the Prophet Isaiah*, chapter 1, verse 18.

71 The hymn is called *Den store hvide flok, vi se* [*The Great White Flock We See*] (1765).

72 In *Dubliners*, 1914.

73 James Joyce, *Dubliners*, Grafton Books, 1977/1986, p. 179.

74 Ibid., pp. 197–8.

75 Ibid., p. 191.

76 Ibid., p. 201.

77 The Dean is quoting *The Book of Psalms*, Psalm 85, verse 11. Loewenhielm reuses this quotation at the beginning and end of his speech 29 years later, as will be mentioned.

78 Robert Langbaum, *The Gayety of Vision – A Study of Isak Dinesen's Art*, Chatto & Windus, London 1964, p. 254.

79 Nietzsche, *The Antichrist* (1895); translated by Walter Kaufmann, The Viking Press, New York, 1954, pp. 572–4.

80 *Last Tales*, pp. 338–9.

81 Ibid., p. 154.

82 Ibid., p. 187.

83 Ibid., p. 188.

84 Ibid., p. 188.

85 Vol. 1, p. 307, from a letter dated 20/12–1939.

86 Leif Søndergaard, *Syv fantastiske analyser af Karen Blixens "Ringen"* [*Seven Fantastic Analyses of Karen Blixen's "The Ring"*] – the title plays on the Danish title of *Seven Gothic Tales*, which is *Syv fantastiske Fortællinger* – in *Kultur og Klasse* 73, nr. 1, 1993, p. 85. In the Danish version of the story, Sigismund is called Konrad; in the quotations here 'Sigismund' is substituted for 'Konrad'.

87 Ibid., p. 87.

88 As told in *Grimms samlede eventyr* [*Grimm's Collected Tales*], Nyt Nordisk Forlag, Arnold Busck, 1987.

89 *Seven Gothic Tales*, p. 329.

90 *Diana's Revenge*, p. 101.

91 "Sildig Opvaagnen"; included in the collection *The Diary of a Parish Clerk and Other Stories*, translated by Paula Hostrup-Jessen, Athlone 1996, p. 153.

92 Ibid., p. 153.

93 Ibid., p. 145.

94 Ibid., p. 156.

95 Ibid., p. 156.

96 Ibid., p. 139.

97 *Out of Africa*, p. 24.

98 *Anecdotes of Destiny*, p. 35.

99 *Shadows on the Grass*, p. 78.

100 Vol. 1, p. 402, letter dated 18/1–1945.

101 *Vinter-Eventyr*, Gyldendal, 1985, p. 91; not in the English language version, *Winter's Tales*.

102 *Out of Africa*, p. 27.

103 And the marriage ceremony quotes *The Gospel According to St Mark*, ch. 10, v. 9.

104 *Kierkegaard's Writings, III; Either/Or, II*, p. 94.

105 Page 242: "She had no object of value about her, only the wedding ring which her husband had set on her finger in church, a week ago."

106 *The Gayety of Vision*, p. 273.

107 *Osceola*, p. 40.

108 Ibid., p. 61.

PART III   LIFE AND TALE

1 *Isak Dinesen: The Life of Karen Blixen*, pp. 4–5.

2 *Digtere og dæmoner* [*Poets and Demons*], Gyldendals Uglebøger, 1959/1973, p. 97.

3 *Letters from Africa, 1914–1931*, p. 110, letter dated 1921.

4 Ibid., p. 111, letter from 1921.

5 Ibid., p. 130, letter dated 4/8–1922.

6 *Aftenpassiar* [*Evening Discourse*], Danmarks Radio, 29/10–1946.

7 *Letters from Africa, 1914–1931*, p. 381, letter dated 13/9–1928.

8 Ibid., p. 209, letter dated 19/4–1924.

9 Ibid., p. 210, letter dated 19/4–1924.

10 Georg Brandes wrote the essay "Wilhelm Dinesen", originally published in *Essays: Danske Personligheder* [*Essays: Danish Personalities*], 1889, and later included in *Danske Digterportrætter* [*Portraits of Danish Writers*], Gyldendals Bibliotek, vol. 17, 1972.

11 *Letters from Africa, 1914–1931*, p. 382, letter dated 13/9–1928.

12 Ibid., p. 245, letter dated 1/4–1926.

13 Ibid., p. 250, letter dated 3/4–1926.

14 Ibid., p. 245, letter dated 1/4–1926.

15 Ibid., p. 245, letter dated 1/4–1926.

16 Ibid., p. 380, letter dated 13/9–1928.

17 Ibid., p. 380, letter dated 13/9–1928.

18 Ibid., p. 244, letter dated 1/4–1926.

19 Ibid., p. 245, letter dated 1/4–1926.

20 Ibid., p. 249, letter dated 3/4–1926.
21 Ibid., p. 246, letter dated 1/4–1926.
22 Ibid., p. 288, letter dated 5/9–1926.
23 Ibid., p. 307, letter dated 13/7–1927.
24 Ibid., p. 407, letter dated 18/5–1930.
25 Ibid., p. 375, letter dated 22/7–1928.
26 *Out of Africa*, p. 25.
27 *Heart of Darkness*, Penguin Books, 1979, pp. 19–20. With reference to *Heart of Darkness* see: Frantz Leander Hansen, "Conrads clairobscur" [Conrad's Chiaroscuro], *Kultur og Klasse* 67, no. 3, 1990.
28 Ibid., p. 106.
29 *Letters from Africa, 1914–1931*, p. 409, letter dated 10/9–1930.
30 *Heart of Darkness*, p. 67.
31 *Shadows on the Grass*, p. 79.
32 *Kierkegaard's Writings, III; Either/Or I*, pp. 288–9.
33 Ibid., pp. 52–3.
34 *Shadows on the Grass*, pp. 80–1.
35 "The Blue Eyes" is an insert tale from "Peter and Rosa" in *Winter's Tales*.
36 *Letters from Africa, 1914–1931*, p. 418, letter dated 10/4–1931.
37 Ibid., pp. 418–19, letter dated 10/4–1931.
38 Shortly before she returned to Denmark, Karen Blixen attempted to take her own life.
39 *Letters from Africa, 1914–1931*, p. 419, letter dated 10/4–1931.
40 *Karen Blixen in Denmark: Letters, 1931–62*, vol. 1, p. 529, letter dated 4/2–1949, written in English.
41 Ibid., vol. 1, p. 193, letter dated 19/7–1935.
42 Ibid., vol. 1, p. 89, letter dated 25/7–1932.
43 Ibid., vol. 2, p. 396, letter dated 18/6–1958.
44 Ibid., vol. 1, p. 166, letter dated 23/8–1934.
45 Ibid., vol. 1, p. 335, letter dated 16/9–1941.
46 Ibid., vol. 1, p. 384, letter dated 3/11–1944.
47 Ibid., vol. 1, p. 335, letter dated 16/9–1941.
48 Ibid., vol. 1, p. 368, letter dated 6/3–1943.
49 Ibid., vol. 2, p. 238, letter dated 1/9–1954.
50 Ibid., vol. 2, pp. 242–3 and 238, letters dated 18/9–1954 and 1/9–1954.
51 Ibid., vol. 1, p. 402, letter dated 18/1–1945. "La grâce de Dieu": the grace of God.
52 Ibid., vol. 1, p. 89, letter dated 25/7–1932.
53 Ibid., vol. 2, p. 453, letter dated 8/8–1961.
54 Ibid., vol. 1, p. 278, letter dated 1/6–1938.
55 Ibid., vol. 1, pp. 276 and 315, letters dated 1/6–1938 and 28/2–1940.
56 Ibid., vol. 2, p. 302, letter dated 6/9–1955.
57 Ibid., vol. 2, p. 396, letter dated 18/6–1958.
58 Ibid., vol. 1, pp. 262–3, letter dated 27/12–1937.
59 Ibid., vol. 2, p. 412, letter dated 17/1–1959.

60 Ibid., vol. 2, p. 112, letter dated 21/10−1952.

61 Ibid., vol. 2, p. 256, letter dated 3/11−1954.

62 Ibid., vol. 2, p. 180, letter dated 4/12−1953.

63 Ibid., vol. 2, pp. 386−7, letter from March 1958.

64 Ibid., vol. 1, pp. 591−2, letter dated 6/6−1950.

65 In a television interview with the Swedish journalist Lasse Holmquist. It must therefore have pleased Karen Blixen to receive a letter from Johannes V. Jensen with the following praise: "What I really wanted to say to you was that to me your writing represents liberation and renewal by encountering composed things, free imagination as distinct from that intolerable self-referential regional literature which currently reigns supreme in this country. The first requirement of a writer is that he or she writes imaginatively, you fulfil this demand completely." *Karen Blixen in Denmark: Letters, 1931−62*, vol. 1, p. 361, letter dated 16/11−1942.

66 James Joyce, *A Portrait of the Artist as a Young Man*, Granada, 1983, p. 154.

67 *Letters from Africa, 1914−1931*, p. 388, letter dated 20/11−1928.

68 *Karen Blixen in Denmark: Letters, 1931−62*, vol. 1, p. 437, letter dated 14/3−1946, written in English.

69 Ibid., vol. 1, pp. 459−60, letter dated 2/10−1946.

70 James Joyce, *Ulysses*, Penguin Books, 1984, p. 374. On Joyce's use in *Ulysses* of Homer's *Odyssey*, see: Frantz Leander Hansen, "Dublin og Ithaka" [Dublin and Ithaca], *Bogens Verden*, no. 2, 1991.

71 Ibid., p. 133.

72 *Karen Blixen in Denmark: Letters, 1931−62*, vol. 1, p. 446, letter from May 1946.

73 Ibid., vol. 1, p. 432, letter dated 31/12−1945.

74 Ibid., vol. 1, p. 293, letter dated 18/4−1939.

75 Ibid., vol. 1, p. 447, letter from May 1946.

76 Ibid., vol. 2, p. 66, letter dated 17/11−1951.

77 Ibid., vol. 2, p. 75, letter dated 15/1−1952.

78 Ibid., vol. 2, p. 77, letter dated 15/1−1952.

79 Ibid., vol. 2, p. 105, letter dated 4/10−1952.

80 Ibid., vol. 2, p. 213, letter dated 13/5−1954.

81 Ibid., vol. 2, p. 418, letter dated 11/11−1959.

82 Ibid., vol. 2, p. 418, letter dated 11/11−1959.

83 *Letters from Africa, 1914−1931*, p. 389, letter dated 20/11−1928.

84 *Karen Blixen in Denmark: Letters, 1931−62*, vol. 2, p. 420, letter dated 11/11−1959.

85 Ibid., vol. 2, p. 310, letter dated 19/10−1955.

86 Ibid., vol. 1, p. 177, letter dated 29/1−1935.

CONCLUSION

1 *Seven Gothic Tales*, p. 170.

2 Fyodor Dostoevsky, *Crime and Punishment*, translated by Jessie Coulson, W. W. Norton & Company, New York, 1964, p. 277.

3 Friedrich Nietzsche, *On the Genealogy of Morality*, translated by Maudemarie Clark and Alan J. Swensen, Hackett Publishing Company, Inc., Indianapolis/ Cambridge, 1998, p.104.

4 *Carnival – Entertainments and Posthumous Tales*, pp. 65–6.

5 *The Antichrist*, p. 655.

6 *Daguerrotypes and Other Essays*, p. 85.

7 *On the Genealogy of Morality*, p. 90.

8 *Shadows on the Grass*, pp. 9–11.

9 Ibid., p. 16.

10 Ibid., not in the English-language version, p. 50 in the Danish version: *Skygger paa Græsset*, Gyldendals Paperbacks, 1992.

11 *Letters from Africa, 1914–1931*, p. 322, letter dated 19/11–1927; "violent" here has the meaning 'wild' or 'untamed', in the positive sense with which Karen Blixen attributes this quality.

12 Ibid., p. 321, letter dated 19/11–1927.

13 Gyldendal, Copenhagen, 1918, vol. 2, p. 270.

14 *Ung Elskov og andre Fortællinger* [*Young Love and Other Tales*], Gyldendal, 1965, p. 380.

15 *Kvinden og aben*, Munksgaard/Rosinante, Copenhagen, 1996. *The Woman and the Ape*, translated by Barbara Haveland, The Harvill Press, London, 1996, p. 165.

16 *Seven Gothic Tales*, p. 43.

17 "The Cardinal's First Tale", *Last Tales*, p. 21.

Published Works by
Karen Blixen

1926 *The Revenge of Truth*
1934 *Seven Gothic Tales*
1937 *Out of Africa*
1942 *Winter's Tales*
1944 *The Angelic Avengers*
1955 *The Ghost Horses*
1957 *Last Tales*
1958 *Anecdotes of Destiny*
1960 *Shadows on the Grass*
1962 *Osceola [Osceola]*
1963 *Ehrengard*
1969 *Karen Blixens Tegninger [Karen Blixen's Drawings]*
1977 *On Modern Marriage and Other Observations*
1978 *Carnival – Entertainments and Posthumous Tales*
1978 *Letters from Africa, 1914–1931*
1979 *Daguerreotypes and Other Essays*
1996 *Karen Blixen i Danmark: Breve 1931–62 [Karen Blixen in Denmark: Letters, 1931–62]*

Selected Bibliography

Susan Hardy Aiken: *Isak Dinesen and the Engendering of Narrative*, Chicago University Press, Chicago/London 1990.

Poul Behrendt: *Tekst, historie og samfund – i Karen Blixens Sorg-Agre*, Kritik no. 41, 1977.

Poul Behrendt: *De forbyttede børn. Tekst, historie og samfund i Karen Blixens En Herregaardshistorie*, Blixeniana 1978.

Svend Bjerg: *Karen Blixens teologi*, Anis 1989.

Thorkild Bjørnvig: *The Pact: My Friendship with Isak Dinesen*, Baton Rouge and London, Louisiana State University Press 1983, translated by Ingvar Schousboe and William Jay Smith. Danish original: *Pagten: Mit venskab med Karen Blixen*, Gyldendal 1974.

Thorkild Bjørnvig, Aage Henriksen, Marianne Juhl: *Karen Blixen*, Spektrum 1992.

Else Brundbjerg: *Isak Dinesen: Karen Blixen: Woman, Heretic and Artist*, Know Ware 1997, translated by Lars Kaaber. Danish original: *Kvinden, kætteren, kunstneren Karen Blixen*, Carit Andersens Forlag 1985.

Else Cederborg: Afterword to *Det drømmende Barn og andre fortællinger*, Dansklærerforeningen, Gyldendal 1979.

Linda Donelson: *Out of Isak Dinesen in Africa: Karen Blixen's untold story*, Iowa, Coulsong List 1995. Danish translation: *Karen Blixen i Afrika. Sandheden bag Den afrikanske Farm*, Ascheoug 1998, translated by Anders Westenholz.

Charlotte Engberg: *Billedets ekko. Om Karen Blixens fortællinger*, Gyldendal 2000.

Susanne Fabricius: Afterword to *Sorg-Agre og Vejene omkring Pisa*, Dansklærerforeningen, Gyldendal 1987.

Bernhard Glienke: *Fatale Präzedenz. Karen Blixens Mythologie*, Karl Wachholtz Verlag, Neumünster 1986.

Donald Hannah: *"Isak Dinesen" and Karen Blixen – The Mask and the Reality*, Putnam & Company, London 1971. Appendix: Karen Blixen: *The Revenge of Truth: A Marionette Comedy*, translated by Donald Hannah.

Frantz Leander Hansen: *Karen Blixens sande historie*, Københavns Folkeuniversitets prospectus, *Sommeren 96*, April 1996.

Dag Heede: *Det umenneskelige: Analyser af seksualitet, køn og identitet hos Karen Blixen*, Odense Universitetsforlag 2001.

Liselotte Henriksen: *Blixikon*, Gyldendal 1999.

Aage Henriksen: *Isak Dinesen/Karen Blixen: The Work and the Life*, St. Martin's Press, New York 1988, translated by William Mischler. Danish original: *Det guddommelige barn og andre essays om Karen Blixen*, Gyldendal 1965.

Aage Henriksen: *De ubændige*, Gyldendal 1984.

Hans Holmberg: *Ingen skygge uden lys*, C. A. Reitzel 1995.

Marianne Juhl and Bo Hakon Jørgensen: *Diana's Revenge – two lines in Isak Dinesen's authorship*, Odense University Press 1985, translated by Anne Born. Danish original: *Dianas Hævn – to spor i Karen Blixens forfatterskab*, Odense Universitetsforlag 1981.

Bo Hakon Jørgensen: *Siden hen – om Karen Blixen*, Odense Universitetsforlag 1999.

Aage Jørgensen: *Litteratur om Karen Blixen. En bibliografi*, Aarhus 1998.

Keith Keller: *Karen Blixen og Filmen*, Aschehoug 1999.

Robert Langbaum: *The Gayety of Vision – A Study of Isak Dinesen's Art*, Chatto & Windus, London 1964. Danish translation: *Mulm, stråler og latter. En studie i Karen Blixens kunst*, Gyldendal 1964, translated by Clara Selborn.

Frans Lasson and Clara Selborn: *The Life and Destiny of Isak Dinesen*, Random House, New York 1970. Danish original: *Karen Blixen. En digterskæbne i billeder*, Gyldendal 1969.

Henrik Ljungberg: *En elementær historie*, Gyldendal 1998.

Mogens Pahuus: *Karen Blixens livsfilosofi: En fortolkning af forfatterskabet*, Aalborg Universitetsforlag 1995.

Grethe F. Rostbøll: *Længslens vingeslag: Analyser af Karen Blixens fortællinger*, Gyldendal 1996.

Tone Selboe: *Kunst og erfaring: En studie i Karen Blixens forfatterskap*, Odense Universitetsforlag 1996.

Clara Selborn: *Notater om Karen Blixen*, Gyldendal 1988.

Leif Søndergaard: *Syv fantastiske analyser af Karen Blixens "Ringen"*, Kultur og Klasse 73, no. 1, 1993.

Ivan Z. Sørensen and Ole Togeby: *Omvejene til Pisa: En fortolkning af Karen Blixen "Vejene omkring Pisa"*, Gyldendal 2001.

Judith Thurman: *Isak Dinesen: The Life of a Storyteller*, St. Martin's Press, New York 1982 (*Isak Dinesen: The Life of Karen Blixen*, George Weidenfeld & Nicolson, London 1982). Danish translation: *Karen Blixen: En fortællers liv*, Gyldendal 1983, translated by Kirsten Jørgensen.

Anders Westenholz: *The Power of Aries: Myth and Reality in Karen Blixen's Life*, Baton Rouge, Louisiana State University Press 1987, translated by Lise Kure-Jensen. Danish original: *Kraftens horn: Myte og virkelighed i Karen Blixens liv*, Gyldendal 1982.

Anders Westenholz: *Den glemte abe: Mand og kvinde hos Karen Blixen*, Gyldendal 1985.

Ole Wivel: *Karen Blixen – et uafsluttet selvopgør*, Lindhardt og Ringhof 1987.

Index

as fundamental forces in life, 11–12, 45,
    47, 50, 141
and Greek gods, 20, 108, 141
in *The Old Testament*, 108, 141
and Pontoppidan, 141
when separated, 11–12, 68, 72
being a fundamental theme, 2, 9, 141
in *The Woman and the Ape* (Høeg),
    141–2
see also demonic; demonisation
Djævlerier (*Diableries*) (Claussen), 78, 103
"Djævlerier" ("Diableries") (Claussen),
    78–9
Don Giovanni (Mozart), 65–6, 87
Don Juan, 65–6, 106, 119
Dorph, Bertha, 8
Dostoevsky, Fyodor, 15, 32
dream and reality, 11, 17, 29–30, 46–7, 57,
    89, 100–1
"Dreamers, The" (Blixen), 15, 51
    and "Babette's Feast", 96
    and "The Dreaming Child", 29
    and "The Immortal Story", 57
"Dreaming Child, The" (Blixen), 29–30
    and "The Dreamers", 29
    and "The Ghost Horses", 33
    and "The Hermits", 29

"Echoes" (Blixen)
    and "Babette's Feast", 96–7
Ehrengard (Blixen), 39–40
    and *Anecdotes of Destiny*, 39
Einstein, Albert, 134
Either/Or (Kierkegaard), 65–6, 109, 116
England
    depicted in *The Angelic Avengers*, 30–2
    Clay ("The Immortal Story") as repre-
        sentative of, 1, 59
    Lamond ("The Heroine") as represen-
        tative of, 26
    see also Blixen, Karen: on England
eroticism, 25, 26, 46, 83, 98, 100, 106–7
    as beneficial danger, 119, 121
    and the devil, 81–2, 105
    and Don Juan, 65–7, 106, 119
    and the Fall, 60, 84, 103, 104–6
    as a fundamental force in life, 140–1
    and Little Red Ridinghood, 102
    in "Tardy Awakening" (Blicher), 104
    see also love; secretiveness; wildness
Essays (Blixen), 40

eternity (immortality)
    the idea of, 2, 3, 100, 134–5, 139, 142
    as the inner plane in Blixen's works, 2,
        143
    acting as theme, 2, 24, 31, 57, 104, 105,
        110
    see also art: the substance of
Europe
    and Africa, 2–3, 13, 123–7, 131, 138, 140
    "Babette's Feast" as a representation of,
        1
    see also Blixen, Karen: resentment
        against Europe of
Ewald, Johannes, 7, 17, 49

fantasy
    and Dostoevsky, 15
    as free imagination, 15, 33–6
    as genre, 14, 36
    the need for, 14, 54
    and reality, 15, 58, 139
    as setting, 15–17
Farah Aden, 140
"Farah" (Blixen), 73, 140
Faru, Wendish goddess, 18
fate. *See* destiny
Father, The (Strindberg), 38
Faust, 65–6
feminine and masculine, 11–12, 17–18,
    100–1, 109, 139
femininity, 17–18, 25, 26–7
Finch Hatton, Denys, 122–3
*Fodreise fra Holmens Kanal til Østpynten
    af Amager* (*Walking Tour from
    Holmen's Canal to the Eastern Point
    of Amager*) (H. C. Andersen), 49
Fra det gamle Danmark 1–2 (*Old Danish
    Tales 1–2*) (Blixen), 98
France
    Babette as an artist in, 69
    Heloise ("The Heroine") as an embodi-
        ment of, 26
    Paris Commune, 7, 69–70, 75, 93, 94,
        95, 105, 117
    as the home of Pennhallow (*The
        Angelic Avengers*), 31
    Virginie ("The Immortal Story") as
        representative of, 59
    see also Blixen, Karen: on France

Gauguin, Paul, 8